TERA'S
TALE

REBEL ON THE RIVER

A life story of
love, rats, cancer,
hoarding, and, did
I mention love?

OTHER BOOKS BY JUDITH ADRIAN

Adrian, Judith & DarRen Morris (2014).
In Warm Blood: Prison & Privilege, Hurt & Heart.
Milwaukee: HenschelHAUS.

Millar, Jackie & Judith Gwinn Adrian (2007).
Because I Am Jackie Millar.
Los Angeles: Golden.

Adrian, Judith Gwinn (1993).
"Reflections of Adult Education: The Field Without a Face."
Unpublished Ph.D. Dissertation.

Madison, WI: University of Wisconsin-Madison.

TERA'S
TALE

REBEL ON THE RIVER

A life story of love, rats, cancer, hoarding, and, did I mention love?

JUDITH GWINN ADRIAN

Henschel
HAUS
publishing, inc.

HenschelHAUS Publishing, Inc.
2625 S. Greeley St. Suite 201
Milwaukee, WI 53207
www.henschelHAUSbooks.com

Ordering Information:
Quantity sales. Special discounts are available on quantity purchases by corporations, associations, and others. For details, contact the "Special Sales Department" at the address above.

ISBN: 978159598-675-7
E-ISBN: 978159598-676-4
LCCN: Pending

DEDICATION

To Tera, Beth and Tom. Thank you for your gentle teachings.

TABLE OF CONTENTS

ACKNOWLEDGMENTS

Tera's Tale was slow coming to completion. The book is a fictionalized biography yet, even at that, preparing it to be told publicly felt like an invasion of Tera's intense need for privacy. I recognize that each of us sees *truth* through our own lenses and life experiences. So, as with my other memoir writings, I believe there is wisdom to be gained by pondering each of our life journeys: the impacts of socially-constructed societal pressures, the decision points, the joys, sorrows and struggles. Tera (no one's real name is used in the book) surely lived all of these.

Write On Door County provided the solitude and space I needed to complete *Tera's Tale* when I finally concluded it was time to tell her story. Tera was there, inspirationally, during the hours where time went from circular to elliptical. (Who knew there were so many hours in a day to reflect and write and rewrite and rewrite again!) *Write On Door County* is a Wisconsin writer's retreat space on close to 40 acres of woodlands and meadows, plus home of writer Norbert Blei's appealing chicken-coop-writing-shed.

So many thanks to those who read Tera's manuscript and offered comments. Each of you have improved the writing and augmented the story. I loved the comment that *I write more than I know*. I hope this is always true. Thanks to Doug Bradley (author, *DEROS Vietnam: Dispatches from the Air-Conditioned Jungle* and co-author, *We Gotta Get Out of This Place: The Soundtrack of the Vietnam War*), Tara Cronin, Larry Engel, Carolina Gwinn, John Gwinn, Bill Harriott, Donna Hart-Tervalon (author, *The Witch's Skin*), Carol Lobes, Tom Nee, Sue Sadowske, and Mark Anthony Rolo (author, *My Mother is Now Earth*).

Special thanks to Neil Heinen for so completely capturing Tera's spirit in the introduction and for introducing me to E.L. Doctorow's *Homer & Langley*, the book that inspired telling Tera's tale.

More special gratitude to DarRen Morris for creating the cover painting for this book (as he did for the book he and I co-authored, *In Warm Blood: Prison & Privilege, Hurt & Heart*) and to Carolina Gwinn for once again transforming DarRen's art into the cover design. You are a deeply talented team!

And last, so many thanks to Kira Henschel (HenschelHAUS Publishers) for your guidance, attention to detail, and help with all aspects of bringing *Tera's Tale: Rebel on the River* to us all. It is time the story be told.

FOREWORD

There is something gently evocative about the notion of one's tale. A tale is an invitation to lift the veil and absorb the wonders of a life ordinary and divine. We often describe a tale as woven; a creation which gives it texture and makes it tactile. There is feeling to a tale. And in the best there are two inseparable contributors, the person about whom the tale is told, and the tale's teller. Tera's Tale would not be the extraordinary, warm, sad, funny, compelling, baffling story it is without Tera and her friend Judith Gwinn Adrian.

Of all the revelatory themes of Lin-Manuel Miranda's breathtaking musical *Hamilton* the one that best explains that tale is the closing song, "Who Lives, Who Dies, Who Tells Your Story." It is an acknowledgement that the degree to which the mystery of any given life is revealed depends on whose story is told and who tells that story. Some stories are never told and lives are diminished or lost. Others join the pantheon of tales that create a collective, if never complete, understanding of what it is to be human.

Adrian has done Tera the honor of telling her story. In the spirit of E. L. Doctorow's equally empathetic story of better known, earlier 20th-century brothers Homer and Langley Collyer, whose bodies were found buried in their impossibly cluttered New York City apartment, Adrian lets us get to know the complex and conflicted person who cannot throw stuff away. The behaviors, communication, physical appearances, all seem a bit odd perhaps, but ultimately socially acceptable; certainly not pathological, or dangerous; until they are. Adrian spares neither Tera nor the reader any of the messy, troubling, often gut-wrenching details of a compulsive hoarder, but she does it with compassion, genuine affection and respect for Tera's dignity and dogged determination to appear to live a normal life. Adrian forces us to confront our own limitations and ask ourselves if we would be able to give the extraordinary gift of friendship she gave to Tera. Think of Sami's teeth in your hand as you answer that question. Think of the rat colony. Think of the procession of dumpsters.

But think too of the heartbreaking sadness of being told "I don't live like other people." Judith Gwinn Adrian's gift is understanding, accepting and caring about people who don't live like other people. *Tera's Tale* is such a gift. It is an honest, unflinching, moving account of an ultimately tragic life that, much like the love affair at its heart, is as revealing as its untold secrets allow us to imagine.

Neil Heinen, Madison writer, journalist and friend

THE CAT BITE

G rit no longer worked. Tera had to acknowledge it. She was undeniably ill.

Tom, her attorney, reported that he drove the few blocks from his home office to the crest of her driveway to create her will.

Hunched over, Tera struggled up her short, pock-marked driveway to the dead-end street where Tom was waiting. As we all were, he was quite aware that people were not invited into Tera's home.

Standing weakly, she dictated her will that the attorney recorded in pencil, writing on the back of the smudged junk mail envelope Tera had given him. The hood of the attorney's car served as their desk.

In her will, Tera entrusted her treasured cat, Sami, to my care as we had long promised each other we would do when (or if) one of us was unable to take care of our pets. (You know...those youthful, well intended, half-hearted, fanciful, unwritten agreements that you never actually, fully imagine will come to fruition.) Tera also declared that most of her estate be used for Sami's care, with an undersized remainder going to her Australian sister.

Tom later said he was deeply uncomfortable with the will as initially written (as was I when I heard about it), but when he suggested alternatives, Tera became screamingly hysterical, in that way she could do. Once in that state she would not—could not—listen to anyone. Only time would calm her.

And it did, calm her that is. The next day the will was rewritten to reflect more measured choices. Tom acknowledged that he didn't know if Tera slept that night after the first will was written. He did not. She looked so ill he was not sure she would live until morning and, of course, her instinct was not to accept help from anyone. She was a fiercely private and independent, even reclusive, person.

A few weeks later, Tera was living in a nursing home and Sami, the treasured cat, had come to live with me. Well, *come* may be too uninspired. Sami had long been living under the bed in Tera's house. To get him out, old boxes had been shoved together creating a narrow passageway—a cat weir. Then, using an ancient toothless broom, hissing-Sami was encouraged into his cat carrier and subsequently, vocalizing duress, came to live with me.

Sami had to be separated from my house cats who cowered at the slightest whiff of his primal scent.

And so Sami, the treasured cat, began living in my garage.

***

It was a perfect July 4, sun-filled and windless. The sky was a blameless blue. The neighbors were out of town and my family was gone for the day. I was in the garage taking care of Sami who had, by now, progressed to living in the large wire mesh dog cage I purchased for him.

He was an eight-year-old, sixteen-pound, intact, seal point Siamese. He had balls and claws and no sense of humor. Unusually long fangs and a serious overbite left him with the scowling look attributed to saber-toothed tigers. Even his fur looked grumpy—thin and scaly.

For a few weeks, I had been trying to build trust between us, but he continued to mostly cower in the darkest corner of the cave-like cardboard box I had put inside his mesh enclosure. His cat eyes darted rapidly from side to side, as he looked out, past me.

"Greasy eyes," my sister said.

I wore fireplace gloves to work with him—the kind worn when picking up burning logs. Sami had once turned and bitten into my glove but was unable to pierce it and had simply let go when there was no response from me, seemingly bored with my colorless reaction.

"Tell me about Sami? How is Sami? I am a cat person. I hate dogs." Tera recited her refrain every time I visited her in the nursing home.

I offered positive Sami-stories as I sat with her in the small darkened cell-like room. Always anxious, she would not join the other nursing home residents for meals or socializing; she did not leave her hot, end-of-the-hall room where she lay on her bed propped against out-of-place colorful stacked pillows mounded in the corner. It was as if she, like Sami, was caged.

Sami received fresh water more than once a day. His litter box was clean. I assumed he was eating the Science Diet cat food I brought him, since it was disappearing, until one day I saw a chipmunk dash into the cage and fill its cheek pockets with the top-drawer cat food.

Sami wasn't exactly eating what I fed him, at least not directly. He preferred his food warm. Fresh chipmunk, a la carte. (Why, I rhetorically wondered, did Sami prefer chipmunk over Science Diet?)

That 4th of July Saturday I clicked the leash on Sami's collar.

"Come on, Sami. Walkies, walkies."

(My parents had once purchased a book intended to help them tame an obstreperous German shepherd puppy. The author, Barbara Woodhouse, had written about taking dogs for *walkies, walkies* and the Irish phrase stuck as a family anecdote. That puppy later chewed Barbara's book into streamers which only added to our merriment around the idiom.)

Before she became ill, Tera daily staked Sami out in her yard using a long, spliced rope. He was familiar with the regular pattern.

That Saturday was a fine day to be free of the cage. He crept ahead of me, seemingly remembering our routine of going to the bushes near the fence separating the neighbor's yard from mine. I fastened his long leash to the fence wire and then worked nearby pulling invasive Creeping Charlie and violets from the edges of my lawn, checking for early tomatoes, gathering peas (I so love those sun-warm garden peas) and plucking enough late season lettuce for dinner.

Sami crouched under cover of the bushes as fit his nature.

An hour later I picked up his leash to return him to his cage. He was amenable and walked seemingly easily ahead of me.

Things were going well. When we got to the garage, I decided to gently brush his fur again. We had worked on that for several days. I was careful to avoid the scabs visible through his ratty fur. I felt we were building trust.

"What a good cat. What a good Sami." I praised him.

After a few minutes, I dropped the fireplace gloves because Sami seemed so relaxed. He was responding to the brushing, arching and paying more attention to me than he had previously.

This was one week before I was scheduled to depart on a six-day bicycle ride. It was my family's second year being part of the fund-raising Tanqueray AIDS rides from Minneapolis to Chicago. I had been in training for six months building up to the nearly 100-mile per day rides that I knew were coming. I had been lifting weights and eating right and was in exceptionally good shape for an olding woman.

But I wasn't quick enough for what happened as I brushed the pale cat fur. I did not see Sami move, much less have time to get away from his long teeth and claws. Without warning, he arched back, bit, and sunk his brown teeth into my right hand. His mouth was so large his lower teeth were in my palm and his upper fangs met them through the muscle above my thumb. The whole base of my thumb was clasped in his locked jaw.

As I instinctively yanked my hand back, he propelled his body onto my arm. He thrust claws into my skin, front claws above my wrist and back claws near my elbow.

In panic, I grabbed the skin on the back of Sami's neck with my left hand.

Deadlock.

The garage was sharply silent. Sami was fastened onto me and I was locked onto Sami. Neither of us breathed and the only movement was my blood dripping in slow motion. I watched, almost detached, as the red drops created a circular polka dot pattern on the concrete floor.

Do you know the feeling when you recognize that you are badly hurt and must make a conscious choice about what to do? My mind raced even as my body moved in slow motion. No one was around; I had to deal with this situation alone. What to do? Part of me was hoping Sami would let go. But it became evident that that was not happening. The blood continued to drip as we knelt, conjoined.

I tried pulling away but he did not relent. Pain was becoming a factor. Pain and shock. I felt I could not let go of his neck, fearful that he would attack my throat or face. He was large and strong and clearly ready to stay locked onto my arm (or body) until I convulsed in death.

I considered slamming him against the studs in the garage wall.

But I had promised Tera that I would save Sami's life.

There was only one other way out that I could think of. I began to pull the cat off my hand and arm. The red spots on the floor multiplied but I kept pulling with the sort of slow determined strength that comes from calculated weight lifting and controlled fear. Even though his teeth and claws did not release, my skin did.

Everything was happening in very slow motion.

When we were separated, I swung him into the open cage. Blood was flowing hard now from four punctures and multiple torn claw sites. I securely fastened the cage door with my left hand. Sami crouched low in the corner of the cage, his eyes locked on mine.

In an abnormally slow, low, and incensed voice, I said aloud, "I bat last."

I knew I had to get help. I went to the kitchen as the blood pattern expanded from the polka dot circle to a ribbon. The cold tap water was soothing, calming. Blood pulsed out as I watched, aware that the spurts were oozing in synch with my racing heartbeats. I wrapped my arm and hand in a large dish towel and went to the phone. I called two friends. No answers. The pink flowers on the towel were turning red. Knowing the local medical clinic was closed for the holiday, I put a second, heavier towel over the first one, got my car keys and drove the eight miles east on the Madison beltline to Park Street, then north to the hospital lot. I parked in a designated visitor's spot (why?) and walked into the lobby.

"How do I get to the emergency room," I asked gesturing toward the towels around my arm.

An efficient volunteer directed me and I walked through the corridors guardedly, hiding the fog and dizziness growing within me.

The emergency room receptionist asked me what the problem was and holding up my arm, I said, "Cat bite."

"Sit down and we will call you," she professionally replied.

I sat, but then couldn't stay in one place. Again, the fear and pain were pounding in my arm and brain. I had been attacked by a wild animal; how could I have so misread Sami? Like Tera, I loved most cats.

I paced around and around the waiting room, past the cheery fish tank and behind the gray plastic chairs. I was an imprisoned tigress. With each circle, my eyes rested on the circling red betta fish as I was thinking about my family coming home to blood blotches on the garage floor.

I watched others with holiday broken bones and head gashes be triaged before me.

One hour.

Two hours.

When a kind nurse finally unwrapped the dishtowels, she said, with slight alarm in her voice, "You should have been admitted to the hospital for this."

My fault, I guess. I should have explained to the receptionist that it was more than a simple cat bite, if there is such a thing. It was combat. It was trauma. But it is my family's way to understate; it is that staid English heritage where even the question, "How are you?" could be interpreted as invading personal space.

The wounds were cleaned. My physician happened to be in the hospital and was summoned. She looked at the rips and punctures.

"Come to my office on Monday," she instructed.

Only later did I understand her worry was that I could end up with diminished hand function.

Two days later, I went to her office and she immediately spotted the red streaks running up my arm. I had not seen the spreading infection and only knew that there was continuing pulsing pain. She called the hospital and had me admitted immediately. I spent the next three days in bed connected to an intravenous-line dripping antibiotics into my arm, which was held in an elevating sling.

During that time, Sami was euthanized.

You see, I was not the first person he had bitten. Tera's Aussie sister had seen Tera's red and very swollen knuckle on her visit a previous summer. Of course, Tera would not see a physician; she only trusted home remedies. And her knuckle did eventually heal. She later wrote her sister, "I am finally healing. I squeezed a cat tooth out of that knuckle."

I did bat last. And I did finish the 500-mile bike ride, with some challenges (antibiotic phototoxicity with intense hand and foot itching).

But, wait, I have gotten ahead of Tera's tale. And my schooling about hoarding.

TERA, JUDY & DOG, FRED

MEETING TERA

My family's first three months in Madison, Wisconsin, were spent in a rental duplex while we waited for our former residence to sell and to find a house we wanted to purchase. The duplex was the sort of place that inspires looking for an alternative. It came complete with oily trails pressed into the once trendy brown shag carpet.

Two things happened simultaneously. I found a small newly constructed blue house on a hillside across the street from a row of old summer homes situated along the river.

And the former house sold.

When we moved in, the road in front of our new house was narrow, two blocks long, and a dead end. It was very apparent that the new row of tract homes, including ours, had cruelly disrupted a quiet hidden old cottage neighborhood. One hundred years before our move, this secreted area had been loved by summer vacationers, as described in a local history book:

> In the early part of the twentieth century...campers, as the temporary summer residents were called, came from Illinois cities like Rockford, Freeport and Chicago.... The cottages they lived in had no plumbing, only an outhouse and a large dishpan for washing utensils. Sometimes there were hand pump wells. The lake served as a bathtub.[1]

Tera lived alone across the street. Her chocolate brown ranch house—built around one of the old cottages—had been lengthened through two small additions and amended by access to village water.

---

[1] Houghton, B., J. Licht & M. Nielsen. City of the Second Lake. Madison: Community Publications, 1976.

When we first met, she was in her early 40s. Tera was shy, veiled, bordering on reclusive, and yet she enjoyed talking with people she knew. Slim and tanned from summers spent outside, Tera looked healthy with natural sun streaks in her long blond disheveled hair. Her eyes were brown and trustingly childlike. From a distance, she was attractive in an uncomplicated, down-to-earth hippy way.

I saw her outside when we moved in that fall. Fred, our schnauzer, and I walked across the road to meet her.

Although she was welcoming, I was surprised to see white streaks on her face running from her eyes to her jaw on both cheeks.

She was working outside so I attributed her musky odor to perspiration. She introduced me to her overweight tan border collie and her cat. The cat was fastened to a tree by varying sized rope pieces tied together. He hid as I approached.

Tera explained at length that she was a cat person but that her dog qualified as a large cat.

"This is the last dog I will ever have," she declared. "I never want anyone giving me any more animals because when I meet them I fall in love with them. I do not ever want another dog. I am a cat person."

I could tell that this was cautionary for me, for the future. No dog gifts (which I would not have done anyway). But it was also the hint of a future relationship since we were now to be neighbors.

After an hour of talking, Tera confided in me that she was distraught about the houses that had been built across the street from her. She had been crying for weeks. I slowly realized that the white lines on her cheeks were salt from unwiped tears. She explained that she and her animals used to walk on the undeveloped hillside where my house and the other eight homes were now standing, offered for purchase by the real estate developer.

"There had been rabbits to chase in the summer and places to cross country ski in the winter," Tera explained. "All of that is gone. And there are new people. Strangers. Strangers to deal with."

This was said without malice, just factually. I did not take it personally even though I was clearly one of the strangers; one of *the other*.

MY FRIEND

I n the early months that Tera and I were neighbors, I noticed the man who came to visit twice a day, every day: every day as in weekdays, weekends, and holidays. He came mid-morning and early afternoon, often right at 1pm. Occasionally he returned in the evening. He brought full grocery bags. He sometimes pulled his boat and he, Tera, and all their pets, including his dog, Tera's dog and the cat in a cat carrier, went for boat rides.

At times he came and they stayed inside her home. Other times he worked outside. Regularly they went away in his car and returned with more bulging grocery bags.

It was probably two years before Tera mentioned him at all. A ghostly figure. Like the cat, he would dart away when I came near. I had no conversations with him in the beginning. Slowly, Tera began to refer to *her friend*. I figured out that the shy man was the friend.

Once I saw Tera and her friend behind the local grocery store. The friend was inside the dumpster tossing loaves of discarded bread out to Tera who was stacking the bread into grocery bags. As I watched from a distance, they filled six bags and put them in the back of his car. (Truly, I'm not normally a busybody, but admittedly this was behavior that heightened my curiosity.)

There were many mysteries surrounding Tera and her life, but I had resolved at least one.

When I asked about the birds on her property, Tera told me she had fed and nursed generations of Canada Geese, Mallards and other ducks. The flowing river water in front of her house did not freeze, so these birds were present and hungry year-round. The ducks and geese had names. (Who knew?)

Tera explained, in detail, "The white one-eyed patriarch with a limp is Hector. His mate, a Canada Goose, is Sally."

MIXED SPECIES GEESE

As I listened, generations of local goose lineages were recounted in laborious detail. (Tera kept a goose journal.) I ended up knowing more than most locals about the solid, big-footed, stocky ancestors of white domestic geese mated with Canada Geese (still living in this area). They are too bulky to migrate. They are Hector's and Sally's progeny.

YUL BRYNNER: THE KING AND TERA

Another summer. I was outside working in my gardens with Fred, the schnauzer. He spotted Tera and rushed, wiggling, across the street to greet her.

Fred loved Tera.

It was mutual even though he was a dog.

I had been paying careful attention to Tera's activities the previous few weeks because I knew her dog had gotten ill and quickly died.

Losing her dog had been occasion for many tearful conversations. Regularly that June Tera sat outside on the steps leading to our front door and talked to me.

"I am a cat person. I do not want any more pets because they break my heart when they die," she repeated time and again.

Fred sat with us and would lean his schnauzer head against Tera's arm as she cried and cried.

The white salt lines again formed on her cheeks.

A few days later, on June 28, Tera appeared on my doorstep to inform me she was leaving the next day, which was a bothersome statement given her mental distress.

Her friend would take care of her cat, she said. "Oh, and I am flying to New York City to watch Yul Brynner's final Broadway performance of *The King and I*."

Little could have surprised me more. Truly. I knew Tera was fascinated with movie stars. I did not know that Yul Brynner was one of her favorites. But still, New York City?! It is somewhat larger than our little village—8.5 million vs. 8.3 thousand.

I wondered then, and will likely never know, how she had gotten a ticket for that final performance. She surely wasn't concerned about the feminist and anti-racist critiques of the play or about British colonial power. She hadn't ever traveled to large cities that I knew of, much less New York on her own. She knew about Brynner's illness though I don't know if she was aware that it was lung cancer or if she was paying attention to his campaign against smoking. I guessed that her interest was in the classic fairy tale romance between Anna and The King and songs like *Hello Young Lovers* that touched the romantic in her.

The next morning Tera loaded a paper sack of clothes into the back of her ancient Ford Fairlane, which actually started when she turned the ignition key. Off she drove toward Milwaukee for her flight, bypassing the Madison airport which is less than ten miles away. I both admired her spunk and feared for her wellbeing as she determinedly left. There was no stopping Tera once she was set on a course of action and I did not try.

A few days later, Tera returned. We did not talk right away because life's events and my studies intervened. But the next weekend, she brought over her already dog-eared and clearly treasured stage bill with *Rodgers & Hammerstein* and the *King & I* printed on the cover. The real highlight, as she pointed to the playbill, appeared to be her mental picture of Brynner standing scantily dressed as the Siamese monarch, legs and arms spread in an imperial macho V.

She spoke of the logistics of the trip. "My car got me to Milwaukee and, with people helping me, I got parked in an airport lot." Continuing to ask directions, she got on the plane and flew non-stop to New York where a compassionate taxi driver took her to the inexpensive hotel that must have been part of the package deal she purchased (or was given) for the play. Ever frugal, she stayed in her hotel room that night.

"I ate the crackers and bread I brought along for dinner and breakfast. A nice doorman directed me to the theater the next day."

Tera adored the play and Brynner, even in his weakened state.

Then she made it back to Milwaukee and part way home.

Tera explained, "My car just began running more and more slowly. It was getting dark. I did not know what was wrong. My car finally stopped on Interstate 94 and I pulled over. Some kind people came by and helped me get home."

Somehow the Fairlane made it back to Madison and into Tera's garage and I feel certain Tera did not pay to have it towed. I doubt that car ever moved again while Tera owned it, at least under its own power.

This New York trip was clearly a once-in-a-lifetime event for Tera, but she and I were impressed with different elements of the adventure. For her, it was seeing Brynner in his most famous play. For me it was the fact that she could pull off such a trip at all.

With the help of kind strangers, she did just fine.

Life can be like that.

OVER THE YEARS

Over the years, when Tera's conversation was not about pets, it was about money. I pieced together that she had retired in her late 30's after twenty years of employment with a local propane company where she had begun working after high school. She had been their clerk/receptionist. She received a small pension along with some additional income from gas stocks.

Tera was amazingly frugal. She had no phone. She had that white, two-door Ford Fairlane that she probably purchased used. And she owned the river house that, I was told later, had been purchased with an inheritance from her mother.

She turned her heat on and off by date rather than temperature: so, on November 1 and off March 1. Even the quixotic know Madison cannot engender seven months of warmth per year.

During actual warmer months, Tera bathed in the river, though she referred to this as *going swimming*, not unlike those turn of the last century "Illinois campers."

With Tera's love of animals, it was reasonable for me to hire her as our animal caretaker when we traveled as a family. She was nearly always home and so we began the ritual of her feeding and patting Fred and our cat, Simon.

I paid her well. And she took very special care of the animals. She left extensive notes about each interaction with the dog and cat. She wrote about every walk, every bowel movement, every feeding, and any other events. The notes were always written on the outside of junk mail envelopes.

Generally, she used one side of an envelope for each day we were gone. Each note came complete with date, time and weather.

2/2 – 9:10pm COLD
Found envelope on my doorstop Monday with "Simon's" key—
note—payment. Thanks!! Simon and Fred looked like they were
expecting me. I read them your note—they looked like they under-
stood and Simon made a sweet low meow—Simon's "look" said to
disregard the "extreme cold part" and just make sure I get here every
day for his food—cute!

2/3 = Hi Judy, 9:30pm still COLD
Simon and Fred at door to greet us. (I got a ride up and back—lucky).
Extreme cold. Also, I hurt left wrist, so was afraid I couldn't get your
"trick" door closed, so my friend did that for me. Fred went for very
short walk. Simon and Fred happy—ate—enjoyed being brushed.
Cleaned cat box. Found your nice "Welcome" note on counter. You
ALL sure know perfect time to leave.

Friday, Feb. 4 2:30pm Fred barking."Simon" right at door again,
happy to see us and their food. (Put mail on counter). Fresh water
in their dish. Cat box. Quick walk. Both enjoyed brushing. (Thank
heavens got my ride up and back with my friend.)

Over nearly a decade, Tera began to trust me. I listened to her stories about her pets. I heard vague references to her friend. She always remembered our family birthdays and anniversaries. On my birthday, January 7, 1986, she copied a quote she had found on the back of a mail advertisement, *What is essential is invisible to the eye. Happy Birthday...the day before Elvis' 51th.*

I encouraged her to use our phone when she required one or to come over whenever she needed help. Her pattern was evident. Each week, on Sunday mornings, year-round, Tera would dress up and get on one of her bicycles (whenever she spotted a bike on the curb that was put out for trash collection she and her enabler (?) friend would bring it home and add it to the line of bicycles that inched around the inner edges of her crowded garage because, she had explained, you never knew when a bike might break down or you would need another for parts). She would ride to the Catholic Church for the service. Once a month or so, she would then ring my door bell after the church service. She would come in only as far as the entryway rug in my split-level house. No further. Together we would sit on the rug to chat.

She would talk. I would listen. Fred would cuddle with her.

***

One summer day, Tera's sister arrived for a visit and Tera brought her to my house. She was so very proud. Words cascaded out of her.

"This is my sister, Beth."

"Beth is a nurse."

"Beth lives in Australia."

"Beth has a fine family. Four children and a great husband."

"Beth has cats."

"Beth is so lucky."

"Beth has *everything*."

Tera couldn't stop the waterfall-Beth-soliloquy. (Beth had everything Tera wanted in life.) We drank lemonade on my deck.

And so the relationship with Tera went season to season, year to year.

MY FRIEND, CONTINUED

Slowly, over the years, I began having conversations with Tera's friend. His shyness, or perhaps it was reluctance to interact with the neighbors, diminished somewhat. Our brief discussions were about Tera's house maintenance or about trees and animals. My family had helped with emergency situations a few times, like the night part of a tree in Tera's yard was split in half by wind or the afternoon the telephone pole transistor next to her garage was hit by lightning causing a rain of sparks and then a fire in the tree branches.

Such events were the gist of his and my talks.

It was years before I knew his name was Hank and years more before I used his name when talking with him. Tera's river-side neighbor seemed to have known Hank in the past and sometimes stood talking with him, both men leaning on the rusty barbed wire fence, laced with wild grape vines which separated the two aged cottage homes.

Hank was a relatively small man, slim and solid in the ways sinewy swimmers are strong rather than exhibiting the bulky musculature of a weight lifter. His hair was unkempt and he did not take the time to shave daily. His face was deeply lined like a man who has spent much of his life in the sun or one who had been a long-time smoker—or both. Details of fashion and color and fabric did not cloud Hank's mind. He exuded the same earthy smells Tera did, like the smells that sometimes come from older people who have either given up on daily cleansing or whose diminished senses of smell incorrectly register the nuances of their own body odors.

I pondered the relationship between Tera and Hank. Once I concluded that Tera's Australian sister, so far away, had hired Hank to come by daily to help Tera survive in her own home. It made sense because he assisted with all sorts of chores from mowing the lawn to cutting firewood.

But then there was their daily feeding of the geese and ducks. And the fact that Hank so often dragged his small rowboat behind the rusted Ford station wagon he drove—the back end of the car filled with sacks of bread and crumbs from former dumpster dives, a dog cage, fishing gear and other paraphernalia for the hobbies and loves he and Tera routinely seemed to share.

My mind would not allow me to view these two-unlikely people (about 20 years different in age) as lovers even though they spent an hour or more in the private recesses of Tera's home each day, every day. There was never any public display of affection between them that I saw. No touches, no looks, not even evident private jokes.

There were the times, though rare, when Tera would rail at Hank, walking around her yard literally screaming at him. One time the shouting was about how he was not helping her but only ruining her life, and her house.

"You are doing more damage than you are worth."

But the shouted comments were never framed in a way that would seriously endanger a personal relationship; rather they were hurled frustrations about inept work or perhaps unmet promises.

The loudest shouting had come when the highway, that ran next to Tera's house, was rebuilt. What had been a lazy two-lane road was upgraded to four smooth lanes. I was home much of that bridge-construction summer, daily writing my dissertation, so heard the one-sided fights.

The crumbling bridge over the river next to Tera's house was revamped into a sleek four-lane concrete and steel passageway that opened a corridor for commuters to glide to work more quickly. Where the bridge had once existed on the same plane as Tera's home,

BRIDGE THAT UNEARTHED CREATURES

encouraging truckers to honk and wave triggering Tera's cheery smile, the new sign of progress sat high above the river and land.

When finished, the bridge blocked views and created far more noise as car and truck sounds echoed off its drum-like surfaces.

Tera detested every aspect of the project from the thundering noise of the pile drivers next to the river to the invasion of construction workers into her very private world. She spent that summer with more salt-stained cheeks and angered cries at the person closest to her, her friend, Hank.

In one of her birthday notes written both to my family and our schnauzer, Tera wrote,

> *Fred = 12, thought of "my" friendly little furry Friend on your 12th birthday, April 18th. Bet you got a lot of extra pats that day.*

> *Hope you all had a nice Easter. Hope Fred's fine; Simon too. Thanks again for the nice fish net gift bag—from Iowa (have it hanging up). Am enjoying the quiet before the noise on the highway work starts again. Love, Tera*

I had known Tera and Hank for around twenty years when I first saw Hank's portable oxygen machine. His dog had died; neither he nor Tera had replaced their canines. The cat, too, had died to more tears and vows of never having another animal because their deaths were overwhelming.

Surprisingly, Sami had appeared at about this time as a shy and reclusive but beautiful cat. A seal point Siamese. He was staked daily in the yard on the long rope and he accompanied Tera and Hank on their frequent boat and car trips, loaded always in the cat carrier that was too small for a cat of his increasing size.

I never knew why Tera accepted this one last animal gift into her life, but she did.

Tera's house was the one closest to the highway and mine the second house away from that noisy road, across the street from Tera's home. Years prior, when we purchased our home, the real estate agent had said, with unblinking eyes, "Sound does not travel up so you won't be bothered by noise from this highway."

One day, in spite of his estimation, I heard the thud of an auto accident near our corner and went out in time to see Tera scampering across the grass to her house and in the back door. Sami's cage swung clumsily as she ran.

On the highway, I could see Hank's car, hit from behind, as he had turned his old Ford into traffic. The new highway bridge had a slight rise to it that was just enough to visually block the entry of his low, slow-moving station wagon.

Tera obviously wasn't hurt. And Hank was moving around OK. The local police were arriving. I did not intervene but did notice that Hank showed up at Tera's home the next day with a different old Ford station wagon, pulling his boat hooked to a shiny new hitch. He also had the strap to a portable backpack oxygen machine slung over his shoulder. Was this accident the beginning of a decline? Was Hank's decline the cause of the accident?

Later that fall I observed that Hank's car was not parked in front of Tera's house as usual when I left for work early afternoon. He was more reliable than any clock I owned, so I was surprised.

And, that night, by chance, I saw his face pictured among those in the obituary columns of the evening newspaper.

Remembering Tera's responses to losing the animals in her life, I couldn't imagine what losing Hank might mean.

Over the course of several days I walked around the log at the crest of Tera's driveway and down the hill to her back door. The beige curtains covering the glass in her door were tightly closed and she did not respond to my overtures. I left tomatoes and squash from my garden as gestures of friendship and concern. They were always gone when I would come by the following day. Clearly Tera did not want to talk and I honored that unstated request. It was several weeks before she reappeared and much later before she mentioned that Hank had come to her house on the day prior to his death.

He never missed a day. Faithful until the end.

In her book, *Peripheral Vision*[2], Mary Catherine Bateson wrote about change. Some people, she stated, tack through life like a sailboat crosses a bay, back and forth, comfortable with the constant change. Others are like the tightrope walker who maintains balance only by changing the angle of the flexible balancing pole. Make the pole rigid, Bateson wrote, and the person will fall.

Tera was the tightrope walker whose routines were always predictable. Each day was as similar as possible to the day before. Each season an echo of the one before. Hank had always come. The ducks were always fed with bread found or purchased. The cats and dogs always joined the boat trips that continued as long as the seasons would allow. Winter was for cross-country skiing. Always. Summer was for reading romance novels on the dock. Noon was soap opera time and the stories echoed her patterns by continuing year after year. Hank arrived at 1pm. In a sense, she lived by natural rhythms like the geese and ducks that were so central to her riverside world.

---

[2] Bateson, M.C. (1994). Peripheral Visions: Learning Along the Way. New York: Harper Collins.

But I think her balance pole became rigid with Hank's death.

Later, close to her own death, she told me, "I did not live like other people." I certainly could not disagree with that statement.

Tera fantasized about the societal dream of marriage and family. She wished for, ached for, the life her Australian sister had. She had stopped time for forty years waiting for the dream to materialize with Hank. But when he died, Tera was forced into realization. She could no longer maintain the patterns or the dreams she had built her life on.

She became even more reclusive.

THE MOVE

One Memorial Day, Tera said, "That house you have always liked is for sale." The small house was about four blocks from where we were living in an area where Tera regularly rode her bike.

I contacted a Realtor the next morning and we put in an offer while the dirt was still moist around the for-sale sign. We hadn't intended to move; we had no thought of moving, but the opportunity was there. Our bid was accepted that same day.

On our anniversary (which was also Tera's birthday) she wrote,

> *Happy Anniversary. (Easy date to remember for me.) Have a good trip Wednesday and Thursday. Time is good for me (found everything on doorstep.) Thanks for pet sitting birthday money. Do have something special planned for it. Thanks for birthday greeting. Will really really miss you all as neighbors across the way—but know how much you'll love the new house. Good luck and best wishes, Tera*

And her gift to me on this occasion was that she took another step toward greater trust. She invited me into her house to see her James Dean collection. I was honored. "Yes, I'd come."

Researchers distinguish between the concepts of hoarding and collecting in that the collector is proud to show what she or he has assembled. Tera was proud of her James Dean shrine! Her collection.

The visit to Dean's shrine was carefully choreographed. The invitation was for just after dusk. No lights were on in the house and Tera led me in through a side door. It was extremely dark inside: I could see nothing other than shadows on the short route we followed.

I could tell there were objects all around me but couldn't identify them. The earthy odors were strong but one was predominant.

It was the unambiguous smell of cat urine, or so I thought.

I also smelled the sweet scent of cut trees and other natural odors. I remembered that Tera burned wood to supplement her heat. We walked a very few steps down the hallway. When Tera directed the flashlight onto the wall I realized I was standing before the James Dean memorial.

"I adore James Dean. I loved him in *Rebel Without a Cause*. This is the poster," she said.

There were several crumpled but smoothed posters and pictures taped on the wall. There were movie advertisements and newspaper clippings. My eyes were just beginning to focus when, abruptly, the flashlight was redirected and turned off. I was escorted back outside.

What I realized through this experience, however, was that I was now in the very tiny inner circle of people Tera trusted. An honor.

As we were packing to move, we held a garage sale coinciding with the community-garage-sale-weekend. To say goodbye to the neighbors, we added a Sunday evening block party to the event, held in our nearly empty garage.

Tera did not contribute items to the garage sale that day but she was a steady purchaser. I gave her many items as well: from a blanket I had crocheted in my earlier days to wool jackets that had belonged to my mother.

Very surprisingly, Tera came to the block party that night. It was a typical neighborhood event including the forty-somethings on our side of the road and mostly sixty to seventy-year olds from the river side of the road. Tera was an anomaly.

She came to the party alone and sat on an unforgiving wooden chair in a corner of the garage, shyly talking to folks who came to her. There was a keg of beer and people repeatedly filled her glass as she sat. (It IS Wisconsin and beer—well, and brandy—are just presumed to be essential to most gatherings.)

She smiled a lot.

I watched over her that night because by this point in our relationship I felt protective of Tera. I wouldn't have admitted that to her, of course, and she clearly did not feel in any way that she needed safeguarding.

On one hand, she was so reclusive I helped protect her privacy by not violating any of her boundaries. She did not want anyone driving a car on her driveway, for example, so kept that large barrier log near the curb. I recognized that that was because the blacktop was deteriorating and she had said she had no money to do the repairs.

On the other hand, in her quiet way she was everyone's friend. She knew more people than I did along our street because she was out walking every day. When there was snow, she walked with her ancient cross-country skis to the nearby park where she skied on the drumlin hills—a mix between cross-country and downhill skiing. When it was warm, she had walked her dog on the leash, like her cat's leash, created from bits of rope tied together.

She talked to neighbors on her walks.

Even visitors to the area knew who Tera was. Often, she sat reading library romance novels and sun bathing on her rickety river dock. The dock was visible from the old highway that passed by the edge of her property. Truckers regularly honked when they drove by, slowing down to meet the reduced speed limit in town. Drivers waved. Catcalls amid cattails. She looked like a blond nymph posed in the idyllic setting of river, weeping willow branches touching the river, framing her. She waved back.

Cities have their characters and special people. Tera qualified on both counts even though most people did not know her full name or her story.

The neighborhood block party lingered on past dark. People were staying and so was Tera. She hadn't moved for more than three hours when she signaled me with crooked finger to come to her. I did. She gestured that I should lean down with my ear close to her mouth. I responded, waiting.

"I have to go to the bathroom."

"There is one right up the stairs"

"No!"

She wanted to go to her home. I did not see what the problem was and said that the party would break up soon and she could leave comfortably now. I could tell by the look on her face that I wasn't getting the whole picture, so I waited for her to tell me more.

She grimaced and haltingly said that she couldn't stand up. I assumed that too much alcohol was the problem and offered to walk with her across the street. Again, I could tell I had missed the mark. So, I waited for more explanation. Childlike, embarrassed, Tera looked up at me from her chair and whispered that she could not hold her urine long enough to get across the street. She had waited too long to move and could not now stand.

Through half-giggled whispers, we developed a plan. I would create a diversion on the other side of the garage while she got up quickly and walked out. She wasn't to try to make it all the way across the street but was to head directly for the thicket of Winged Euonomyous bushes framing my driveway and there quickly crouch and let loose.

And so I did. And so she did.

When I looked back, no trail of urine marked the floor. A few minutes later I saw her wave impishly from the middle of the street as she made her way back home.

***

My family had moved the four blocks away and Tera continued to stop by some Sunday mornings. She was always available to take care of our animals when we traveled. She had watched our son grow from a three-year-old to a man and often spoke of how lucky I was to have a good husband and fine son.

Most of her conversation was about Sami and how special that cat was to her and about what would happen if she ever became ill or died. Who would take care of her beloved cat since she had no family nearby? She and I made a pact that I would be her cat's caretaker if the need ever arose.

Tera was serious about her animal-sitting responsibilities. Because she had no phone, I would mail her a note or leave one under the mat at her back door asking if she could watch our cats (Fred and Simon had both died by this time and been replaced by new cats). She would ride by on her bike with her response. I do not ever remember a time when she said no to these four or five requests yearly.

My family was making our annual trek to Chicago for Thanksgiving and Tera had agreed to watch the cats. We left on a Wednesday afternoon after work and returned Sunday to find that the cats had been drinking water from the toilet and had bitten open the plastic bags of dry cat food I left on the counter for Tera, divided into the needed daily amounts.

I was so shocked that Tera would not have taken care of the animals that I dropped my suitcase and immediately drove to her house, fearful of what I would find. I knocked and knocked again, more loudly; waited and then knocked again, with determination. Finally, Tera's face appeared framed in the narrow opening of a curtain pulled aside. She slowly and awkwardly opened the door.

She looked extremely pale and ill.

She stepped out onto the back porch and I saw her right arm held out straight and swollen to the size of her thigh. Her skin was purple and so tight I could almost feel the heat and pain. I offered to immediately take her to the emergency room, but Tera had her own ways of dealing with things and would not hear of my interference. She said she was treating this problem and would be better in a few days. It had happened before, she said, so she knew how it would progress. (She did not remember that she was supposed to have taken care of the cats that weekend and I did not mention it.)

She did agree that I could bring some hot food for her and permitted me to stop by the next day and the next. Of course, I did not go into her house.

Only later she told me that it was her cat, Sami, who had bitten her and that the resulting infection had caused *some swelling,* as she put it.

It took a long time for this injury to heal but by the Christmas holidays, Tera was eager to do more cat sitting saying the income helped her purchase the gifts she wanted to buy and send to her sister, Beth and family in Australia.

THE PHONE CALL

The phone call came on a Wednesday night.

It was from our former neighbor who reported that Tera had come asking to use his phone. She wanted to call her attorney to make out her will. Seeing her weakness and pallor, he had insisted on taking her to a local medical clinic. Surprisingly she agreed. At the clinic she met briefly with a physician.

The diagnosis was cancer.

This did not make sense to me since I did not know how a physician could determine a cancer through a quick visit, but I didn't challenge it.

The neighbor called me that Wednesday evening to say this was his busy time at work and he could not help Tera the next day when another appointment had been set up, this time with a cancer specialist.

He pleaded, "Can you drive her tomorrow?"

Two other calls came in that same evening and it was decided that three of Tera's friends would accompany her to the specialist. The other two women were strangers to me and to each other, but we met at the specialist's office at 2pm, as agreed, after one friend picked Tera up at her home.

Tera needed a wheelchair to get into the waiting room and sat with her head bowed on her chest, her unwashed and straggly blond hair hanging over her face. Because she was so profoundly uncomfortable, socially and physically, we four sat huddled in a circle at the far end of the waiting room. By 4pm, we decided the room was aptly named and it was nearly 5pm before Tera's name was called.

We asked if she wanted to see the physician alone. She did not. So, the three of us walked across the empty waiting room, pushing

Tera in her wheel chair down the medicinal smelling hallway. We squeezed into the small examining room.

The physician had no smile lines at the corners of his eyes. He held a thin folder in his hands as he entered the room and bruskly sat down at eye level with Tera.

She would not look at him.

He asked her some questions about her general health. She mumbled answers I could not hear and then she abruptly asked to leave, to go to the bathroom. A nurse helped her do that while the rest of us sat silently and uncomfortably in the crowded examining room. The physician opened the thin folder and reread what was written there.

When Tera returned, the physician bluntly commanded, "Unbutton your blouse."

Tera very slowly did as she was told. She wore no bra so when the final button was undone, she dropped her arms to her sides and sat passively, inertly, with the shirt covering her chest.

"Open your blouse," the lab-coated stranger demanded.

I was sitting directly across the small exam room from Tera, behind the doctor. Tera looked straight at me as if we were alone in the room. With her dull eyes still staring into mine, she slowly exposed her breasts.

I did not look down but held Tera's eyes. She clearly needed reassurance and I was the person in the logical physical position to give it.

But, my eyes could see a wider picture even as I held on to her submissive trapped stare and I saw the blur of a large reddish-brown stain covering all of one breast, part of her chest, and angling down her arm.

The physician looked quickly, did not touch her, then told Tera to button her shirt. He began to fire questions, insensitively.

"How long have you had this? Why didn't you come in sooner for treatment? You do know what this is, don't you?" he demanded.

It was as if he did not want to have to be accountable for what he saw; what he knew.

His tone became more and more badgering as he tried to get a response from Tera; tried to get her to take some responsibility for her illness. My discomfort was moving to fury. How dare this man abuse Tera? Could it possibly matter whether she had known what her illness was? Why couldn't he see that Tera was unique and special, childlike? Why couldn't he understand that tenderness would go further than this harassing approach?

And then he stopped the rain of questions and gave Tera some sample bottles of antibiotics and told her to wait outside with the nurse.

After she left the room, he turned to the rest of us and blurted, "She has the most advanced breast cancer I have ever seen in my career as a cancer specialist. I have only read about cases like this and those did not happen in Wisconsin, but in the deep rural south or Appalachia. She will need nursing care. She could be given chemotherapy but only to slightly prolong her life. She will die within a few months."

The words were spoken matter-of-factly and without emotion or compassion.

My anger with him actually helped because it somewhat dulled the shock of what he was saying.

Although I knew this was happening to Tera, I could not help relating it to myself. I was afraid. I suddenly understood the neighbor's reluctance to step further into this situation. I realized I was committing to a condition that would take much of my coming summer; the first one I'd had free since beginning my ten years of graduate study. "Selfish," I said to myself.

And then I felt the fear that I was to feel repeatedly in the coming months. I don't know exactly what it was. A fear that the disease would spread to me? A fear of seeing Tera in uncontrolled pain? A fear of the unknown of what lay ahead? A fear of death?

It turned out one of the women in our little band of Tera's helpers was a longtime friend from high school. After the shock of the doctor's visit she stepped forward offering to take Tera to her home at least for the short term. I was impressed. None of us felt Tera should return alone to her house that day but neither had the other woman nor I offered our homes. Tera was in a stupor and it was the next day before she could tell us her sisters' names.

I did not know Tera had two sisters.

The other sister lived in Green Bay, about 60 miles away. She was contacted. She came to Madison by the week's end, after work, and spent Saturday night with Tera, back in her house by the river. I stopped at the house that Sunday morning to see if all was going okay.

The sister walked toward me, welled with tears and fell into my arms, crying. I held her without asking why she was crying, assuming it was her sister's health crisis.

But later that day she contacted Tera's high school friend and asked her to pick up Tera again. The sister could not stay in that house and she could not help Tera.

I never saw her again.

Tom, Tera's lawyer, had information on the Australian sister, Beth. Through an Internet search he found a phone number for her. A call was made and Beth said she would get on a plane immediately and fly to Madison. During the days it took to get that accomplished, Tera continued to live with her old friend who provided regular meals, shampoo, soap, and companionship. Tera's spirit seemed to lighten, especially with the knowledge that her beloved Beth was coming.

BETH

eth arrived. I think the ragtag group of strangers who had been helping Tera was pleased and relieved to give over the responsibility for decision making to a medically trained, caring family member. Beth was deeply weary from the days of travel involved in getting from far Western Australia, to Madison. The challenges she faced immediately were enormous. Foremost, however, was greeting her dying sister who was awaiting her arrival, counting hours, minutes.

"Next thing I'll do is get Tera's house set up to accommodate a hospital bed and other nursing equipment. I will care for her in her home," Beth declared

The idea seemed good to me and I'll admit to again selfishly thinking I could back away from this difficult situation and give care and decision making over to Beth.

Slowly though it became apparent that the plan for taking care of Tera in her own home would not work and that Beth, too, had to live elsewhere. I wasn't clear about what the actual problems were and Beth was not forthcoming in explaining other than to say that she had to find places for them both to live.

"An apartment perhaps," she softly explained.

So, the ragtag support group did not step away, but stayed to help Beth find the services she needed. We each took a piece of the problem and began researching solutions. Lodging. Continuing medical care, including the decision about chemotherapy or no chemotherapy. Should Hospice be involved? Cat care. (Looking back, I realized that no one had taken care of Sami while Tera was living with her former classmate.)

Beth had been away from the U.S. for 25 years. Aboriginal midwifery had become her Australian medical specialty so her knowledge of advanced cancer care was dated at best. She also knew nothing about the contemporary U.S. social services system. She was steeped in and expectant of the same kinds of medical care readily available in her adopted country with its high-level safety net for health and medical issues. Clearly, she needed help and she took what I thought was a courageous path and one that assured my loyalty.

She asked for my help.

What seems so simple may be one of our most difficult human actions, at least in western culture. Reaching out to a stranger. Vulnerably admitting the need for help. But then, as I thought about it, this was what Tera did when she took the Yul Brynner trip. She trusted that the universe would help her when needed, and it did—people did. The universe can be like that.

And so my summer became committed to helping Beth help Tera.

***

Beth was a kind woman with warm eyes and joyful laugh lines. She was paradoxically both a bold take-charge person and an easy-going woman who got distracted by irrelevant details as readily as a chipmunk sniffing out peanut butter in a maze.

As I came to know her I could easily imagine her, as midwife, tenderly caring for young women in labor, her older, slightly pudgy, hands unswervingly caressing the new mom's wet hair reassuring her that the struggle was going to be worth the outcome. And if things did not go well, I can think of few people I'd rather have around to help wade into grief.

With deep-rooted superstition and a strong sense of the preposterous, Beth told me that one of the first things that happened to her as she returned to U.S. soil was, "A bird shat on me head."

Once I translated *shat* I got the essence of the story. From that moment on, most of the time I was with Beth that summer she wore a dirty crumpled baseball cap partly covering her unkempt reddish gray curls. She explained that she found the cap near Tera's garage and so, pragmatically, put it on. And, honoring the fact that George Strait was Tera's favorite singer, Beth also donned a sweatshirt displaying his photo and album name "Lead On" that she likely found somewhere in the house or garage.

BETH WITH HER FOUND-HAT

I was seeing parallels in these two sisters' down-to-earth problem-solving abilities. Tera would have put that found cap on for the same reason. And she would have worn it all summer as well in case another bird headed her way, so to speak.

Over that first week, as Beth transferred her nights to days, decisions were made. Beth rented a room in a private house that was biking distance from the small nursing home where Tera had been moved. Beth found the row of ancient bicycles in Tera's garage, selected the most viable one, and got help to pump up the tires.

Slowly a daily routine began to form. Beth spent her mornings with Tera in the nursing home and her afternoons at Tera's house. At first, my visits were to the nursing home where we would talk as a trio. Tera was clean now and lying back against the bank of bright pillows Beth and I had purchased at a local discount store to add some warmth and color to the barren room.

The first monthly chemotherapy had happened and Tera was extremely nauseous at first then later well enough to occasionally walk outside with Beth and sit on the strangely sterile and unkempt veranda of the small nursing home where, otherwise, she always stayed in her room at the end of the hall not interacting with the other nine women who lived side-by-side in their own separate spaces that were decorated with objects reminiscent of their former full lives.

Tera's room was bare. Her withdrawn lifestyle continued even in the nursing home. I have no doubt she was the object of much curiosity and talk.

Someone sent Tera a plant with a solicitous card bidding her a speedy recovery. She bellowed saying the plant needed to be removed from her room.

"I hate plants," she unpretentiously screamed with her head lying low on her chest and a pink plastic tub nearby to catch the frequent vomit that slid from her mouth following the second chemo treatment. "I am a cat person."

There was now a ragged hand-scratched list of names taped to the outside of Tera's nursing home door announcing that she would only allow certain people to visit her. My name was still on the list, but regularly names were roughly crossed off when I would arrive. (Who were these people?)

Tera's smiles came when Beth was present. Sitting with the sisters for an hour or so on different days, I began learning about their shared childhoods.

Their stories set the stage for what was to come.

THE HOUSE

On my first visits to the nursing home, Tera talked of her cat, Sami, and Beth whispered about Tera's house. Beth was feeling overwhelmed by the challenge of helping her sister and preparing the house for whatever was to follow. She could not bring herself to admit to Tera or to herself that that place would never be *home* again. But at the same time, Beth knew that at least some cleaning needed to be done.

The Aussie charm and frankness had won me over and I volunteered to help with some of the house cleaning as well as visiting Tera. Or perhaps I just told myself this and was actually helping with the house because I did not know what to do with or for Tera.

My first day of volunteering to help clean at the house, I walked down the familiar driveway, passing the log that kept cars off Tera's crumbling blacktop.

To my right was the small grassy area near the highway. Cars and trucks rumbled past on the completed four-lane bridge crossing the river within yards of Tera's house. The truck drivers no longer honked at Tera sitting on her rickety dock. The stack of firewood, several full cords deep, lay molding in the humid Wisconsin air behind the detached garage. I remembered having seen Hank place fallen branches and sticks on that pile after summer storms. This had been the wood, I knew, that Tera used to supplement her home heat.

There was the unchanged single platform step covered with once-green indoor/outdoor carpeting by the back door. I knocked on the door, feeling the familiar give to the wood beneath me and peered at the faded beige opaque curtains covering the small window.

I could hear the usual staccato Canada goose and duck calls coming from the river.

Beth came to the door and half shut it behind her as Tera had always done. Then she slowly turned, without comment, and opened the door fully.

She stepped aside.

Standing there, breathing and looking in was a sensory experience. Intense musky smells, half-remembered from my one-time visit to the James Dean shrine, surrounded me even as I stood in the doorway. Sprayed cat urine was the strongest but not the only smell; the other odors were indistinguishable to me.

The door opened into a storage area, likely once called a mudroom. It was a space where boots might have been lined up below tidy coats hung on orderly pegs. Now it was a maze of objects stacked nearly to head height. Next to the door was a large box that I have since recognized as the kind 4H youth take to county fairs when they are showing their prize animals. It was about three feet high and deep and then four or five feet long.

Behind the box were stacks and stacks of folded grocery store bags and on top of it were rows of bags filled with stale bread. Sweet bread mold was part of the mix of odors.

The brown tiles on the floor were checked and broken so my shoes touched the patchy merger of wooden sub-flooring and scattered shards of tile.

From this narrow space, Beth wordlessly led me into the kitchen area. To my right, I glimpsed what had once been the living room with a picture window facing toward the river. We wound our way into the kitchen following the narrow walking path.

Things were stacked high on both sides.

In the kitchen, I saw that every counter space was covered with glass bottles and jars. Long unwashed dishes were stacked high in both sinks and on the gas stove top.

KITCHEN, PHOTO TAKEN AFTER MUCH CLEANING

Letting my eyes linger on the bottles and jars I realized they were all filled with water (or some other liquid) and stacked three and four high on the counters.

Beth continued to lead me. We turned right. She was silent, as though we were walking into a church or a shrine. I was silent too. The flooring under my feet was very uneven and I tried to watch where I was stepping but the light was dim and there were few alternatives on the narrow pathways.

We moved from the kitchen through a hallway stacked with canned goods and newspapers. Everything was orderly. We moved into the dining area, which gave me full view of the living room.

Although there were a few pictures on the walls, the floor was overloaded with objects and so was the unidentifiable furniture. There was only one place where a person could have been seated and that was on the window seat near the large picture window overlooking the river and the geese. The seat was piled with stacks of newspapers, but there was room enough for one person (and one cat) to sit in the afternoon sun.

In the dining room area, the odors were stronger. Tears came uninvited to my eyes. I wanted to cover my nose but could not insult Tera in her distant bed or Beth who was furtively watching my reactions, my movements. The dining room table and all surfaces were covered with objects. I noticed tall stacks of empty cups—paper cups from fast food restaurants. The stacks leaned, just short of falling over, but not by much. Next to them were tidy stacks of hundreds of straws in paper wrappers. And next to that, lids. Lids from disposable drink cups, from yogurt containers, from ketchup bottles and more. The lids were confined to many, many plastic containers, again stacked high. And next to these, piles of napkins with neatly squared corners. Everything was arranged by category.

I thought about stories of people who lived through the Depression and how they often gained a scarcity-mentality of save-everything-because-you-never-know-when-you-might-need-it. And I thought of my (take no prisoners) grandmother's home where, as small children, we entertained ourselves by surreptitiously and soundlessly playing with the rubber bands we found on doorknobs throughout the house. It was as if they were always in place in case something needed binding or controlling.

Continuing through another narrow passageway in Tera's home, we came to a relatively large family room. In front of the stone fireplace was a stack of firewood about four feet high and six feet long. It was the width of a single bed. Atop the woodpile were layers of blankets and a pillow. Later, after seeing the bedrooms, I realized that Tera slept on this woodpile that served both as her source of heat and her bed frame.

Again, I felt my feet teetering on the uneven surface as I shuffled along behind Beth.

To our left was a 1930's style wall covered by hand-crafted built-in glass fronted knotty pine cupboards. Inside the cupboards were rows of books and papers, stacked and piled to fill all the spaces.

We wound down the hallway. To the left was the bathroom. Floor tiles had long ago released and were resting randomly, water stained and broken, around the floor. There were more jars filled with clear liquid and the tub was level with water that would have spilled on the floor had even a bar of soap been added. Buckets and sponges and stacked cardboard boxes of unopened lotions and cleaners and soaps lined the floor under the sink and around the toilet. Each type of soap or lotion had its own separate box.

BATHROOM, AFTER EVERYTHING WAS REMOVED

There were three bedrooms down the hallway and as we began to walk that direction I realized I could easily see daylight through the rotted bottom of the side exit door that Tera had used to bring me into her house on my single previous visit.

There were beds in the first two rooms that were stacked high with clothes.

Large boxes lined the wall spaces and they too were stacked with clothes neatly laid out in like piles—dresses, sweaters, slacks, blouses.

There were no open surfaces.

BEDROOM WITH CLOTHES

The door to the third bedroom was closed and Beth indicated that Sami, the cat, had lived in that room. She opened the door.

The thick smell of cat urine burst out at us. Part of the ceiling had fallen in and was resting on the piles of clothes.

BEDROOM WITH CEILING FALLING IN

There were cardboard litter boxes, filled with newspaper, in a line along one wall that had been used so many times the soggy sides sagged. Still silent, Beth then turned and led me back on the path through the kitchen space and outside. There she stopped. I had not wanted to touch anything in the house. I felt as if I had entered a ghostly edifice that was laced with something deeply evil, something unidentifiable, and I breathed with relief to be back outside. Suddenly I understood fully the pained hug I had gotten from Tera's Green Bay sister. Now I understood why Beth had said she could not bring Tera home to her house to live out the last months of her life. And I saw why Beth, too, could not stay in this place.

I felt ill. I saw no way to deal with the scope of this chaos. The first thought that came to mind, once I could breathe again, was to burn it all. Second was to bulldoze the whole structure into its own basement. Save nothing. Nothing.

But Beth saw a completely different reality.

For her, the house contained a plethora of childhood memories. Her mother's dining room table. Her aunt's rocking chair. Family books and albums. Her grandmother's sewing basket. Family treasures were hidden like nuggets among the piles. And Beth wanted to salvage these things—these memories—to ship back to Australia.

THURSDAYS AT TERA'S

t was Thursday and as Beth and I stood talking on Tera's buckling driveway, Tom, who had prepared Tera's will, writing it on the hood of his car, drove up to help with the work of cleaning. He had a bag of donuts with him, and coffee. The three of us stood and ate. Geese chattered nearby. We drank our coffees and then we three began what became, for a while, the weekly ritual we referred to as "Thursdays at Tera's," our play on the book, *Tuesdays With Morrie*.

Beth spent afternoons, as she came to spend nearly every week that summer, sorting. On Thursdays Tom and I would arrive early, eat our donuts with Beth, don our disposable surgical gloves and begin carrying the garbage and recyclables that Beth had sorted out to the curb. The garbage truck came about 3pm and by then we had lined the 100 feet of curb with sack after sack of garbage and barrels and bins of recyclable glass and tin and newspaper and plastic. This work slowly widened pathways in the house.

We were a small, but trustworthy, work team. Beth was embarrassed at the state of the house and would not allow others in. She was protecting her sister even though death was inevitable and there were no other family members in the immediate area that would ever know the stories. When curious and well-meaning neighbors or friends came to the door, Beth stood, as Tera had always done, blocking the view and talking only on the sagging stoop.

One deeply curious neighbor came and tried to see into the house, around Beth. All she could spot was a yellowed, mildewed picture of a field of sheep hanging on the mud room wall. She said, "Oh, I have always loved that painting. Could I purchase it from you?" Beth agreed to the sale and set the price at $100, cash. The woman returned with the payment, hoping to get inside the house, I believe. Her ticket of admission. Beth met her at the door and handed over the humidity-curled, paint-by-number picture, took the money and said her goodbyes.

I smiled to myself, very certain that the woman had never been in Tera's house and never would be.

But the weekly Thursday display of recyclables was attracting local attention.

In those early weeks, Beth sorted papers. It seemed Tera had saved every letter she had ever received. Forty years of letters and photos were stuffed in the knotty pine cabinets and stacks of boxes on the family room floor. Beth sat on an overturned metal tub, wearing her baseball cap, reading and making slow decisions about what to save. For her the time became a reflection on the past, her past as well as Tera's.

Each week when Tom and I arrived, Beth would talk about her childhood experiences. She wanted to tell the stories. We would work and listen. Carry a bag of garbage to the street. Listen to Beth tell a story. Carry a box of papers to the curb for recycling. Listen to Beth read a letter.

The stories helped me understand Tera. They helped me understand Beth and their Green Bay sister. Every envelope, every corner in the house held memories. The journey into her past was hard, sometimes horrific.

Much later, at the summer's end and after Beth had returned to Australia, I sent her this manuscript, written with her permission. She responded with more detailed information in several long letters. She wanted me (and you) to better understand the background for her struggles with the house, with Tera, with the past and their present.

Here is some of what Beth reflectively wrote.

We were three girls on a small dairy farm in south central Wisconsin in the 1930's. We hated it. Why? A bit of background may help. Our parents were vastly different. The only 'glue' was our parents' Eastern European ancestry, the Roman Catholic religion, and their similar ages.

Our mother grew up in a vocal and crowded family in an immigrant neighborhood in Chicago; the second to last child of a family of eight. She went through her second year in high school and did stenographer work at the Chicago stockyards for about ten years. And then she just quit and stayed home until her marriage.

Our father grew up on a farm near Friendship, Wisconsin, the oldest of ten children. His parents moved to Wisconsin because Minnesota [near Little Falls] was deemed too cold. Father's mother, our grandmother, was a domineering Polish woman who married an older man and produced ten children.

Our parents met while mother was vacationing at a small lakeside cottage near Father's farm. They were both 35 years old and decided this was a last chance for marriage and a family. The only real date we heard about was going to the movie Birth of a Nation. *Mother loved movies and my father seemed to detest anything that wasn't work related.*

At first my mother loved the openness of the country. But the isolation, lack of meaningful communication with my father, and lack of social interaction soon took its toll. There were plenty of social events in the area, just not for us.

My father was able to purchase the farm near Westfield because it was the depression AND the previous farmer had hung himself in the woodshed. It was only about 30 miles away from where he grew up but, in reality, could have been the other side of the world for all the times we visited his family.

As Tera once pointed out, if everyone else had lived the same as we did, it would not have mattered so much. But they didn't. Our farm was in a Protestant belt. Our schoolmates' parents were all younger. We DID not have running water, ever, while we lived there. We rarely left the farm. My father would take over chores while neighbors vacationed but would never ask for the favour to be returned.

There were three years of wedded bliss before Tera was born on the 4th of June 1934. Our parents were apparently very joyful and if Tera had been an only child, they might have been able to cope. However, three years later a sister arrived and 16 months later another sister arrived and in between a miscarriage and a stillbirth.

After 3 years of Tera being an only child, the pattern was set. Tera threw tantrums to get what she wanted so it was always Tera and the two of us—the other two sisters.

Our pattern growing up was, Saturday night grocery shopping in Westfield, with only one real store in town. Sunday was always ten miles to church/mass in the closest Catholic town and ten miles home—such a boring mass, so long in the hot Wisconsin summers. We children had to fast before mass. No breakfast. Only water. I remember nearly fainting by the time it was finished.

I did not like/love our parents and could never admit that to anyone for a long time. We were brought up with great guilt through our parents and the Catholic Church.

It is hard to explain just where our feelings of shyness, inadequacy, self-consciousness came from, except from what I said earlier: Older parents who acted old and considered themselves Eastern European even though they were born in America. My parents acted old and dressed old if that makes sense. Everything was conform and do not think outside the square. Girls were only useful as potential housewives and mothers. We just grew up with that. My mother's greatest ambition was to see us married off to handsome successful men without giving us the confidence in ourselves to attain that.

We were Catholics surrounded by Protestants. There were lots of Protestant churches in the town. The village with the closest Catholic Church was ten miles away. The other kids had a readymade social outlet every Sunday and other times, like holidays. This was a time when Catholics were not to enter another church. Or if we went to a wedding, there was no singing or joining in prayers. Families were broken up by people marrying outside the church, we were told.

Our social interaction was limited, except for school. There was no positive feedback. My father would have preferred boys to girls for the farm. We received very limited attention and no attention to psychological needs. We received plenty of criticism, but no praise or credit for anything.

The abuse was emotional, never physical. My mother rarely stood up to my father because he had a loud and explosive temper. His temper did not happen often but when it did, everyone knew. He was a silent man anyway and would from time to time stop talking to my mother and ask us to pour his coffee. That made us feel like we were betraying our mother. There was such a cold feeling in the house.

To give Father his due, he gave my mother a driving lesson once. He put her in the paddock [field] with the car. After a feeble attempt, she threw up her hands and said, "I can't do it," and never touched the car again.

It would have made a huge difference in our lives if she had driven. My father would have let my mother take the car to socialize and take us places. He hated having to come in from work and drive us anywhere. One time my mother insisted we go to a movie. We all went. Mildred Pierce *[a bad choice] with Joan Crawford, I think. Mildred, a woman who did not live by the rules.*

Father walked out half way through and drove us home, zigzagging all the way. Three miles. It seemed like forever. He was showing his disapproval.

Growing up, Tera wanted all the attention, all of the time. Anything where choice was involved, Tera had to be first. In high school, Tera probably achieved average grades but she had no ambition for further education.

She was very possessive of her things. Tera hated the competition from our cousins when they came to visit [rarely]. They got tired of talking about movie stars all the time and Tera would go off and bang a door shut until the house shook.

Our sister and I played together and did not include Tera. We ganged up on her too; touching her books and things. We just wanted to see her get mad.

Beth' stories were stunning to me. I had known Tera for many years and had spent hours with her talking about dogs and cats and money and occasionally "her friend." But I knew virtually none of this past. So much made sense. The strict adherence to Catholicism. The parallels with her mother's life of being a secretary and then quitting early, as Tera had done; working just long enough to qualify for a pension. The love of movies and movie stars was evident. The reclusiveness and Tera's acceptance of a house without running water or, eventually, heat. The tantrums I saw and heard as Tera would explode at her friend for not maintaining her house properly or sufficiently.

But centrally, what I saw was the reality that Tera could never achieve her dream (or her mother's dream for her) of marriage and a family.

As I would learn later, Hank was married and had a family. Their affair lasted 40 years. Tera apparently always thought he was going to start a new life with her.

It never happened.

I heard that Tera attended Hank's funeral; his family had to have known about her. Had to. But such a relationship wasn't proper and did not fit family mores. Hank had to be kept secret. A lifetime of secrecy. I often think about the cultural and societal rules we live by and how we live (and die) by our parochial social constructions. Something I suppose Mildred Pierce would have revolted against.

Did Tera's inability to live her dream lead to what was uncovered in her house? Maybe.

***

Thursdays at Tera's continued but it became evident that no real progress was being made.

Attorney Tom and I changed gears.

It would have taken a decade to clean the house at the rate it was progressing.

Beth was reluctant to accept the fact that Tera was not going to come home again. She did not want to disturb her things. In addition, Beth was still spending much of her time reading every letter and card and notebook in the built-in knotty-pine bookcases.

Decades of history.

Finally, one Thursday, over donuts and coffee, we had a serious three-way talk—Tom, Beth and I. If the house was to be emptied, focused removal had to begin.

Tera was not coming home, ever.

Beth knew this, at one level, and finally, reluctantly acquiesced.

Also, the waste company had begun complaining about the quantity of trash and recycling we were producing. They insisted we get a dumpster. Beth ordered the first (of eventually four) full-size dumpsters. Each one was placed on the driveway, further breaking apart the old blacktop. We got good at hurling objects over the tall sides.

Thus began a new, more focused phase in the cleaning process.

Our cleaning days expanded. No longer just once a week. While Beth and Tom worked in the living room, I started on the kitchen, still trying to recycle some of the objects (we later gave this up). A cardboard box could hold 10 or 20 glass jars. I began pouring the water out of the jars into the sink but quickly realized the water was not going anywhere. The bottles had to be taken outside and dumped. The water was stale and some jars would not open. They had been sealed long, perhaps for years. Slowly I worked my way back to the wall behind the counter tops.

One day I spotted a variegated arch of colors on the white splashboard as the last of the jars was removed nearest the stove. It was not a full pallet of colors—charcoals and grays and browns only. It looked as if someone had taken a stiff and nearly dry two-inch paintbrush and painted a partial circle on the wall.

Behind the next group of jars was another similar arc. They continued across the wall, undulating, as more surfaces were uncovered. When I moved the jar nearest the corner, I heard a rustle in the wall. I leapt back but when there was no further sound, I returned to the jar and moved it just far enough to see a large hole in the drywall. It was the size of a small grapefruit. The gray-brown streaks ended at the hole.

I did not think overly much about this since so much in the house was in disarray and so continued with the jars. But when I moved the next group of jars, there were more streaks on the wallboard and another hole, actually a pair of holes this time. These were oval shaped and stacked one on top of the other like eggs standing on their points. These were smaller holes, closer to the size of an orange. I was puzzled but continued to work until Beth and Tom joined me and we examined the unfolding pattern of streaks and holes.

ANIMAL TRACINGS IN KITCHEN

Realization came to us about the same time. The undulating wiry brushed brown streaks, the piles of dirt, and the holes with well-worn edges were the back roads and passageways of an animal that was living in the house. A fairly large, wild animal.

In one of the letters Beth sent after returning to Australia, she wrote more about houses, starting with the farmhouse she and her sisters grew up in:

> No money was ever spent on the farm house. ANY money went to the farm. We had a nice dining room suite and hope chest. My mother spent her last personal money on those items and we grew up hearing, 'Never give your money to a man.' But we had no life skills to go with that recommendation.

> Growing up, the farm house was never totally tidy but never as bad as Tera's. It was an old house with a closed off parlour. There was no carpeting and no furniture to speak of. The kitchen was basic. The

stove was wood until much, much later. There was only an icebox until I was about eight years old.

None of us three girls became tidy housekeepers and our excuse was we were needed for farm work. To this day I prefer outside to inside. We were and are all hoarders and so was my mother.

The cold feeling from the house came because there never appeared to be any warm greetings or easy conversation. As long as my mother was left alone we had lots of freedom. But we had to be absolutely quiet when father came in to sit and listen to the radio, eat meals, or read the newspaper.

Beth's writing then turned to earlier visits to Tera's house:

Tera's house was bought around 1971-1972, after Mother passed away. She bought the house on impulse because of its location and I don't think anything would have made her change her mind even though someone could have told her the foundations were not right and that water kept getting into the basement.

I visited Tera in the house in 1973-1974. It was my first trip back to the states with my husband and three children in tow. And I was pregnant. The first thing I noticed was that the house was very musty and dusty. I put it down to the closed-up winter time. Other than that it was in good condition and spacious. Very light and bright. Tera agreed to turn the heat up for our January visit but I had to agree to pay for it. My Australian husband could not believe we were expected to exist in that cold temperature. I cannot remember exactly what the furnace was set on, but it was LOW.

I loved waking up to the hum of traffic going across the bridge [before the traffic became so heavy] and looking out of the bay window at the river and seeing the muskrat swimming along, the mist over the water, and, of course, all the ducks. Big John was my most memorable duck because he was tame and I held him for a photo.

We had a big open house while we were there for relatives and friends. Our Uncle Alex had great delight in coming to me and saying, 'Did you do all the cooking and preparation?' I said, 'Yes.' He said, 'Tera can cook you know!!' I said I knew that but it was easier on everyone if we just let her keep pretending she couldn't. I also paid for all our food for daily use to the point and in THAT pantry everything basic was marked with our names, Tera or Beth. This became an issue when my number one son fractured his leg in Milwaukee. I stayed in Milwaukee to be near him and my husband came back to Tera's house with other two children. He was trying to do the cooking and Tera would be looking over his shoulder in the pantry and saying, "Which flour did you use??" [Are you laughing yet?] We did share lots of stories during those months AND I was ready to go home and was never homesick for snow or Wisconsin again [almost].

The next time we visited the house was years later. Happily it was summer. I reassured myself thinking at least it will not be musty or dusty because all the windows will be open and the breeze will come. That was such a huge shock. I walked into the house and could smell what? More musty than ever. I nearly cried and did later. Tera said she was looking forward to our visit for over a year. We [husband and two teenage daughters] finally arrived late evening tired and emotional [having visited other relatives first in Friendship, Wisconsin]. Tera lived without a telephone so we had no way of contacting her with our arrival time.

Later, I found these words in one of Tera's diaries: "Beth and family came here last after I was waiting all day. I am still last on everyone's list. Like always."

That made me feel really bad because it wasn't true. Also, one step in that house and I knew we couldn't stay. I could have but would not subject my family to it. Tera ran around the house and into the dog's bedroom saying, "This is where the dog died. Did I change the sheets or not?" while lifting up a corner of the covers. I cringed! God knows what was going through my husband's mind or our daughters'. Eventually our daughters dragged mattresses out into the middle room and slept there. Husband and I went to back bedroom which looked and smelled the best. As I put my tired head down on a pillow, I thought I saw a stain on the pillow [mouse urine]. I eventually went to sleep from sheer exhaustion and woke up the next morning crying. I just wanted to sit there and cry and cry. Mostly I felt sad that Tera lived like that and expected us to as well. I knew we couldn't, especially when Tera started following my husband around with a bucket and saying, "Do you want to do number one or two?" He said, "Where is the nearest shop?" We went there and went to the toilet.

There were sealed sweet rolls on the table and Tera is saying, "Is this the human food or the duck food?" That was enough to make me go on a diet.

This is when we met you, Judy.

Tera took us across the road to do so. You kept saying, "Tera must be so happy because your visit is all she has talked about for a while." All I did was feel full of guilt knowing I was making arrangements to get away from there as fast as possible and stay with friends during our remaining time in Wisconsin. We were on our way to North Carolina for almost a year. Our daughters just had this resigned look on their faces. From the time we hit California, one daughter had wanted to stay in the states and kept saying, "I'll stay with Auntie Tera."

That changed in a hurry.

The overwhelming smell in the house was mouse urine. I will have that smell with me for the rest of my days. I can immediately iden-tify it anywhere. I did write Tera a letter from North Carolina trying to explain my feelings and my sadness for her and wanting her to respond to it. She wrote regularly but never mentioned that letter until she was sick and I was coming back and she said, "Beth is coming over to torch my house!!"

THE NURSING HOME

Beth had purchased some comfortable pink-flowered cotton pajama bottoms for her sister to wear in the new, clean nursing facility Tera had been moved into. The pajamas were large for Tera but did not constrict her as she tossed on the extra firm institutional issue bed. Tera said the pajamas were comfortable but too loose and so she dealt with this problem as she had creatively resolved many problems. She put on the pajama bottoms and then wore her underwear over the top. The look was not fetching but the fit was admittedly good.

About two weeks after the first chemotherapy treatment, Tera began to feel better. We were expecting that she would lose her hair from the drugs and to ease that transition, got agreement from her to cut her hair shorter. Tera had not had a professional haircut in years. On the day the hair stylist came to the nursing home, Tera agreed to a hair wash and blunt cut. The short style fell just below her ears. She looked beautiful. Her hair was sun-streaked blond. As she wearily lay back in her bed I looked at the exposed length of her naked leg. I saw firm, freckled skin and taut muscles. How could she look so healthy when I knew she was so ill?

Tera glowed in her sister's presence. There were girlhood stories. There was sisterly teasing. Beth rubbed her feet. She brushed Tera's hair. Beth changed the bandages covering the seeping breast. I wondered if such patterns of care had begun in girlhood, in spite of the estrangement.

Do abused children comfort each other in special ways?

Beth wrote about Tera as a girl:

In grade school Tera did have a best friend named Caroline. They would actually visit each other's houses to play and talk. Tera got hooked on movie stars and radio stars. This was fine while they were children but then came high school. Caroline grew up AND moved to the high school town where she was able to participate in everything. I think somehow this is where Tera got locked into teenage years. She never outgrew her obsession with stars and movies. Her high school years were years of loneliness, acne, nerves, anger, and jealousy. She had no self-confidence. There were no dances. No proms. No sports. She was agonizingly shy.

With Beth as my guide, I began to physically touch Tera though touch had never been part of our relationship. I was uncomfortable. The combination of my personal awkwardness coupled with the lingering fear of the disease was present and yet through Beth's patient kindness I began allowing myself to press beyond that. Here was a dying woman who needed comfort. Who was I to withhold that because I was overly apprehensive?

At first my touches were light and short. But I learned and later, even after a nurse rushed in one day to tell me not to be near Tera because she was septic, I donned (now familiar) gloves and pushed past discomfort to continue the caring strokes. It was soothing for us both. I imagined myself in Tera's position and asked what I would want. Touch. Authentic caring. Teasing and laughter. All were present with Beth's tender teaching.

By the end of her first month in nursing care, Tera had most of the names roughly scratched off the visitor's list on her door. Mine remained and I am sure it was only because I was Sami's caretaker. I brought regular cat reports but it wasn't enough. Tera wanted to see her treasured friend.

Sami was used to having the leash snapped onto his collar, so it was relatively easy to move him from the large cage in my garage back into the small one that had been his home for boat rides with Tera and her friend. I draped a towel over the cage when I put him in my car for the ride.

Tera wanted to hold Sami. Beth and I were afraid to open the cage door (afraid that Sami might bite Tera), so told her it was against the facility rules to free him. She accepted that ruling then quietly pointed out that both of them were caged. I did not know if she was referring to the narrow lives they were each living or to the disease and treatment confining her and the wildness confining Sami. The assessment was accurate either way.

The visit was unsuccessful. Sami was not the cat Tera remembered. The caretaking I was offering him was traumatizing, as was the unfamiliarity of Tera's sober institutional room that smelled of urine and fear. He would not respond to her in any of the ways she wanted and finally she stopped trying and turned toward the wall that someone had painted with what they deemed to be a soothing pastel green. Tera was not soothed. Tera was distraught at having seen Sami in his estranged state. His health was the topic of conversation for the next week.

On that fateful Fourth of July, Beth borrowed a car with the intent of taking Tera out to see the evening fireworks. Tera's mind was more focused on her cat than on fireworks, so it was arranged (unbeknownst to me) that there would be two destinations for the trip. The first would be to see Sami in his garage home—my garage—and the second to the highest hill in the area for fireworks viewing.

I had just returned home from the hospital emergency room. My hand and arm were bandaged following the cat bite treatment.

Seeing Beth and Tera drive in to the driveway panicked me. I knew that there was the circle of blood on the floor in front of Sami's cage. I asked my husband to greet the surprise guests while I darted into the garage with towels. The blood was long dried so I dragged the metal cage forward on the rough concrete garage floor to cover the stains, not even looking into the cat's eyes. I knew the raspy sound and motion would terrorize him even further but saw no way to fix that. The cat was no longer my real concern.

I stood with my bandaged arm held behind me, out of sight, as the garage door was opened and Tera struggled over to the cage to see her beloved cat. He was unresponsive and she stayed only a minute in front of his cage before slumping into the borrowed car and angrily demanding that Beth drive back to her room.

I had failed Tera. I hadn't kept my promise of taking care of what she loved most in the world (well, next to Beth of course).

And even worse, Sami had bitten Beth before he bit me. I did not know this. She had gone to another hospital emergency room. She had spoken nurse-to-nurse about her injury and gotten rapid treatment. She was horrified that I too had been attacked. The difficult decision was made that this wild animal had to be euthanized even though Beth had already gotten a microchip implanted in Sami's back so he could later travel to Australia with her.

My husband and Beth took Sami to the Humane Society on the Monday after the Fourth of July while IV antibiotics flowed into my arm in the hospital room.

And so it was done.

THE AIDS RIDE

Thursday morning I was released from the hospital with mega doses of penicillin pills in tow. Sunday was Day Zero for the bike ride that would last through the following Saturday. Over 2000 people converged in Minneapolis for the orientation and preparations preceding the 500-mile fund-raising ride to support AIDS research and education. It was my second AIDS ride, so I knew what to expect and how to avoid the long lines that entangled first year riders. My arm and hand were bandaged and still swollen but I was convinced I could complete the trip and set out riding south along the Mississippi River on Monday morning at 6am with the others. Day One was a ride of just under 100 miles. The riders were jovial and the growing camaraderie that energizes such an event was forming as people helped each other with calls like, "Car Back!" and "On Your Left!"

Being one of the olding riders, I knew that that second call was one I would hear all day in actuality and all night in my dreams for the next week as others passed me.

Such a ride is a group and an individual experience, with much time for personal reflection. I found myself thinking about Tera and Beth. Had I done the right thing in insisting that Sami be euthanized? Why was I having to push myself past Tera's disease to touch her when she had been nothing but trusting and kind to me throughout our relationship? Was I spending more time with Beth and the house cleaning because there was something tangible to do there and it was much easier than dealing with Tera's slow sure death?

As a person almost obsessive about cleanliness and neatness, was I sickened or disgusted by Tera's house in ways I could not address or admit to? Was I judging her?

At the end of AIDS Ride Day number one, my arm was swollen and throbbing, but tiredness and heat were larger factors, so I ignored it.

Day Two we began the back-roads' ride across Wisconsin that was the highlight of the trip in terms of natural beauty. Again, spirits were high although some riders were limping and had bandaged knees already. The morning was Wisconsin summer cold so I slipped on the tights I had brought just for such an occasion. I wore them to the first pit stop at the twenty-mile mark and decided to leave them on to the second rest stop.

When I dismounted my bike at mile forty, I knew I had made a mistake in putting the tights under my biking shorts (I should have taken a lesson from Tera and put them on the outside!). They had rubbed against too tender hipbones and literally worn holes on both sides of my rump. I stopped at the medical tent to ask about this problem. The nurse said she could put Tough Skin on the wounds but we needed a private place to do this.

The only alternative was one of the portable toilets. Embarrassed, we squeezed inside and I stood on the toilet seat, pants around my knees and bending over toward the poor woman who was inches away from my sweaty posterior. She was putting on bandages that would still be there two weeks later. It isn't called *Tough* for nothing. Standing there, dim with humiliation, I thought of Tera as she faced the cancer specialist with his brutal questions.

Rather than the battering Tera had received, I had the kindness of a nurse who reassured me that she had seen posteriors before though not quite in this same position (we laughed) and that she volunteered for this job because the AIDS fund raising we were all doing was so important. How different Tera's experience and mine.

The hilly Day Two ride had been just over 80 miles and that night my hands and feet tingled from the exertion. My rump did more than tingle, but at least I did not have an ace bandage around a knee like so many others. That sort of an injury could end a rider's participation and I wanted to complete the full 500 miles.

Camaraderie had been building among the riders on Day Two. Walking our bikes, single file, through the candle lit mile-long tunnel on the Sparta-Elroy Bike Trail, a rider ahead of me called out, "Car Back!" Much laughter. And then silence and darkness. Water was dripping from the ceiling of this former railroad tunnel. I thought about death and burial. Would it feel like this to be buried? Cold. Dark. Damp. In the silence of my thoughts another rider began to sing. *Amazing Grace.* He had a trained, mellow gospel voice that echoed through the length of the tunnel. No one could see the tears that rolled down my face (perhaps creating white salt streaks). It was the first time I had cried since Tera's diagnosis. I did not know what the tears were for. Tera's abuse? Tera's impending death? Tera's ignorance, poverty and fear that had blocked her from getting early treatment? Beth' strength and kindness? Violating Tera's trust in killing her cat? My pulsing arm and burning rump? The growing horror of the house cleaning?

Maybe it was all these things.

In the evening of Day Three, it became apparent that more was wrong than I was permitting my brain to register. The itching on my hands and feet was so intense I just sat in my tent scratching, right through dinner and it isn't like me to miss a meal! I used my toenails to scratch my hands at the same time as I was using my fingernails to scratch the bottoms of my feet. And when all was raw, I limped to the medical tent, hoping to find the kind nurse who carried *Tough Skin* in her white lab coat pocket. The volunteer Ride-physician looked at my bandaged arm and my red hands and feet and asked if I was taking antibiotics. A drug reaction. "Stop taking them immediately," he commanded. The itching had subsided by morning.

Day Four. Driving rain and cold. Combine that with tail end of the of central Wisconsin hills and the bike ride became the measure of a person's character. Many riding with us had orange triangle flags on the backs of their bikes indicating they were either HIV positive or had AIDS. They needed to be marked for medical reasons; it had been explained to us. But it was also evident to all of us that fighting a bit of cold, wet wind, and moraine hills was nothing compared to what others on the ride were having to go through…to what Tera was going through in her darkened cell.

This trip was a family experience. My son was part of the motorcycle crew assisting riders in trouble and providing support at busy intersections. On the day of the cold rain, he came up behind a rider who gave him the thumb-down signal that meant *rider in trouble*. The bicyclist had an orange flag on his bike. Standing next to his bike, he was shivering badly.

Nearly in tears, the bicyclist said, "I cannot finish the ride. I wanted to so badly. But I am just too cold."

Only a few words were exchanged. My son pulled off his jacket and gave it to the man, explaining that with the motorcycle he could easily stop somewhere and get warm. The bicyclist was able to continue riding.

On Day Six we all rode into Chicago through busy traffic to the downtown Loop. At Grant Park, the riders were bunched together, given rainbow colored T-shirts and we rode en masse to the dramatic closing ceremonies near Buckingham Fountain. Families, supportive volunteers and riders assembled in a huge swarm. There were temporary fences in place to help direct people and traffic.

As my family and I watched, a lanky man stepped over fences and wound his way through the crowd toward our son. He was carrying the jacket lent on the rainy day. The jacket passed from one hand to the other and then, at first tentatively and awkwardly and then with honest affection, the two men—one straight and one gay, with AIDS—hugged each other, long. Just like touching Tera, I tearfully thought. Moving beyond artificial fears.

LIES AND LYING LIARS

The week we had been biking, Beth had moved into our house. She had taken a vacation of sorts too, a vacation from cleaning Tera's house. She continued her morning trips to the nursing facility but spent the afternoons and evenings visiting with family and a cousin of hers who was passing through from the East Coast.

I surprised myself at my relief in seeing Beth happy and relaxed. Before telling stories from the AIDS Ride, I wanted to hear about her week's experiences. And she told me in detail as the two of us huddled intently, intimately, on wooden chairs, in a corner, hands resting on each other's knees, away from the noise of victorious voices celebrating the return home.

We had both temporarily escaped the problem we knew we faced. It was: *should we tell Tera about her cat's death?* Beth voted yes. Cowardly, I voted no. My assumption was that Beth' vote was worth more than mine, so we agreed to tell the truth.

Tera was nauseous following the second chemotherapy treatment, but we wanted to end the fabricated cat stories thinking that would bring us some emotional relief.

Later, we sat at the common room table in the nursing facility getting the details correct on our story and knowing that Tera was likely to erupt in anger and sadness. The facility administrator joined us, uninvited. She pointed out things we knew but seemed to have forgotten. Tera was dying. Tera was feeling very ill. Tera was reclusive and non-responsive to most people. We were among the few people she trusted. The administrator helped us see the pointlessness of telling Tera the truth about this one facet of her previous life she continued to hold on to. She helped us see that we were thinking more about ourselves than we were about Tera.

And so Beth and I became the lying liars who told Tera about Sami's move. I took the lead saying that it was evident Sami was just too sad living in a cage in my garage. He missed Tera so much. I said that I had arranged that Sami be moved to the northern part of the state where a Siamese breeder wanted him as a stud cat because he was so beautiful and strong and smart. I said that I was checking on him—the cat, not the breeder—weekly by email and that he was strutting around feeling quite sassy already. I said he had acclimated to the change and was far happier than he had been continuing to live with me. I brought pictures I had taken of Sami in my yard for her to see his "new home."

It was the sort of story Tera wanted to hear and whether she believed me or not, she played along. And so began the regular stories about Sami, the stud cat, that I wove in increasing detail.

But lying to Tera changed our relationship. I could not be as authentic as I had been with her and, from my perspective at least, trust faded. I had more and more trouble facing her and as she lost her hair and became ever sicker and more distant, I wasn't there for her in the ways I had hoped I could be. What I did do though was move my allegiance to Beth. More and more time was spent cleaning Tera's house. Ironically, the house cleaning proved to be another test of courage. But so far, I was not all that proud of my mettle.

Beth was again spending her mornings with Tera at the facility and afternoons reading and sorting. More stories emerged. Talking about Tera's fear of hospitals and doctors, Beth later wrote,

> *Tera's great fear of hospitals and doctors probably started when she was about four years old. At that time our Aunt Pauline died in childbirth with her third child. It was probably from a haemorrhage. Tera remembered the overwhelming grief surrounding her death with everyone talking and not noticing her taking everything in. And then there was the funeral with uninhibited sobbing and sadness.*

As a child, Tera also went through a life-threatening bout of whooping cough. She was bedridden with it for about four weeks and off school about six weeks. She could only sit in bed and cough and cough and turn purple with the effort. One of the few times the doctor came to the house, and he came twice in that time, he took one look at our other sister and I who were also coughing, but active, and said, "Nothing wrong with those two."

Tera was driven to school by our father her first day back. That was also almost unheard of. All the children from our one-room school house came running up to the car. Tera said that we stood in the doorway and watched her cough and choke, only making it worse. I only remember that we were fascinated and horrified and frightened.

And then there was the near-drowning episode. In the hot summer days we were allowed to walk the mile and a half to the local pond to go swimming. None of us were taught to swim so we just mostly played around. Tera got into deeper water and screamed; our sister jumped in to help. Like a drowning person does, Tera latched on and pulled her under. The thrashing and screaming seemed to go on for ages. There was a business nearby and a grandma who used to come out and tell us off for making noise playing around. But this day NO ONE heard or came out to help. I was shouting by this time too, as a six-year-old might do, and holding a thin and ineffectual stick in the water. I really thought my sisters were going to drown in front of my eyes.

Our sister's version of how it ended was she saw a figure of a man standing on the bank saying, "You can do it. Come on. You can make it!" I can tell you there was definitely no one there that I could see and I was looking and praying for someone to appear.

WILD ANIMALS

Reflecting back, I did not quickly understand the significance of the holes in the drywall behind Tera's kitchen counters. I can be remarkably naïve. From that one rustling sound, I thought I had heard, I concluded that a large animal was living in the walls of the house and was somewhat uncomfortable with that. But we were cleaning things out and any creature was surely going to leave soon if that hadn't already happened with the disruptions we had created on the kitchen counter and in the whole of the house.

Tom and I continued to work together in the kitchen area that one particular day.

When all the kitchen counters were cleaned off, we had a clear pattern of holes at every corner, often more than one, and the wire brush looking streaks arching along the wall. There were eight or nine openings visible.

Now that there was open counter space we decided to start moving dishes out so Beth could look at them and begin making decisions on what would be donated to Goodwill and what she was going to pack up to sail to Australia in the cargo ship container she had reserved.

Opening the first two cupboard doors felt like we had entered a Halloween movie set. Cobwebs stretched and then broke as the doors were opened. The hinges squeaked. The cupboards were both piled high with glasses, which wasn't surprising since we were discovering that Tera always grouped like-things together. We wanted to wash the glasses, or at least rinse them. As dirty as they were, Beth could not tell which ones might have come from the farm—from the childhood she and Tera shared. Washing the glasses meant stacking them in baskets or boxes, carrying them into the bathroom and washing them in the standing water in the bathtub. This procedure only lasted part of that day because the standing water could not drain away and quickly got extremely dirty.

All of the bottom cupboards were equally spider web coated and we worked slowly through the stacks of bowls and plates and cups, each in their own cupboard and each one filling every possible cupboard corner.

After we gave up washing the dishes, we began dusting them and then stacking them on the counters for Beth to sort through later. Tom and I wore our surgical gloves as we worked in the house, but for the dusty dishes, we sometimes added surgical masks. Even with all the windows opened, the dust created a thick fog at times. When we got to the backs of the cupboards there was evidence of more gnawing on the wooden backing, but no actual holes. There was no space inside the cupboards for anything other than dishes.

We had picked up our cleaning pace because Tera was getting progressively more ill; the job needed to be completed. The next day I got to the house early and set up a ladder to reach the upper row of cupboards. I tugged on the first door but it would not come open. I repositioned the ladder and tugged more. No movement. A screwdriver rested on the pile of tools we had assembled on the dining room table and I got it to use as a pry.

Not wanting to damage the knotty pine cupboard surface too badly with the screwdriver, I gave up on the first cupboard and moved on to the next one. Same problem. It was a humid summer day in a humid summer week and Wisconsin cupboard doors do swell. I tried the third door and felt some give. With one foot on the ladder and one standing in a small space on the kitchen counter, I pulled hard and the door swung open. I nearly fell off the ladder at what greeted me. It was as if I was looking at the inside of a beehive, but the creatures that had created the hive were not bees. I was looking, I realized, at *underground* tunnels created by burrowing animals that had brought dirt and sticks and leaves and grasses into the cupboards and created a highway of den areas. It occurred to me that perhaps all of the cupboards were linked through the holes in the kitchen walls. And when Tom arrived and pulled open other upper doors, that was exactly what we saw—a maze of animal tunnels and dens etched with brown animal fur.

My first thought, again, was to burn the whole house. It reminded me (okay, well slightly) of the time my mother had discovered a mouse in her car glove box and teasingly but seriously demanded, "Sell it!" (The car, not the mouse.)

ANIMAL HOLES IN ENTRYWAY

I am not an overly squeamish person, but this look at the tunnels was unnerving. I also knew that the animal or animals that lived in the maze had been around very recently. The tunnels were clean and hard packed. No spider webs had formed.

Beth wanted to know what sorts of family heirlooms might be in the upper cupboards and so, with shovels and rakes and toothless brooms, we began to dig out the burrows. And, as she anticipated (or remembered from her last visit many years prior) there were old family dishes woven into the mud jumble. Another awareness came to me as we dug. The animals that had created the burrows were not mice. They were larger than that; significantly larger.

Speaking of mice, though, they too lived in the kitchen. We found their homes as we opened the drawers below the counter. They had taken newspaper and pieces of cloth from dishtowels and hot pads and created their own spaces in the silverware drawer, the towel drawer, the plastic bag drawer, and the cooking utensil drawer. Drawer space after drawer space was literally level with mouse nesting.

Days were spent digging things out and putting them in piles on the counter and stove top and tables for Beth to sort through.

And my nights were spent with the sorts of dreams that left me awake and feeling startled and uneasy. The inside of the stove was mouse nest heaven. And the refrigerator? Well, no creatures had gotten in from the outside so what was in there had grown on its own. My guess was that it had not been opened for one, maybe two years. It just continued to slowly grow the organisms that could survive inside that warm moist box. There was no way to identify what foods had once been in there.

Day by day decisions were made. More large holes were uncovered as we worked in the living room and the den and the family room area. Other than that *scurry* on the first day working in the kitchen I had heard no other evidence that any animals still lived in the house.

Newspapers were stacked in one of the smaller bedrooms—Sami's room—where the ceiling had fallen in. It took two days to move the papers out into the dumpster. We had given up on recycling at this point and were on our second extra-large dumpster.

Once the rug was uncovered in that room I could see why the flooring had felt so uneven. There were layers of rugs in that area and in each of the rooms and hallways throughout the house. Two of us rolled up the first rug with its layer of dirt and shredded newspaper. Under it was another rug with another inch of dirt. And below that, a third. I examined the dirt and discovered it wasn't only dirt. It was also mixed with animal feces, mouse droppings perhaps.

The house was feeling horribly haunted and had it not been for Beth's request for help, I would have fled the situation. But how could I leave Beth with all this work to be done? The living room awaited us with its shoulder high pile of wood for the fireplace and then two other bedrooms stacked high with clothes.

In such a situation, character is tested and although I hadn't been one of the helpers with the refrigerator cleaning, which Beth had done alone, I was persevering. That was, until we came to the dining room closet.

I did not know there was a closet in the dining room until we had moved stacks of furniture and more newspapers, but slowly the door became visible. We were accustomed to the holes gnawed in corners now and not surprised that the closet door had gnaw markings along the bottom as well. The odors in the house remained unbearable at times and there were moments when I would go outside just to breath freely without the mask. But as we uncovered the outside of the dining room closet door, the smells were the strongest we had encountered.

I remembered the day I had gone into an egg-laying barn on an Iowa farm. Tiny wire chicken pens were stacked ten or twelve feet high. There were channels for eggs to roll down. The smell was blinding and I had to leave the barn in spite of a desire not to embarrass the proud farmer who was showing me his egg-laying operation. There were similarities between these two situations because I knew Beth was deeply humiliated by what we were uncovering and yet had to continue the process of, literally, digging out.

As had become the norm with doors in this house, the living room closet door was stuck. Beth, Tom and I pulled on it and then tied a rope around the doorknob so we could get a better purchase. Three of us pulled and tugged.

HEART OF THE COLONY IN LIVING ROOM CLOSET

When the door finally flung open, I first saw only darkness. The smell was overwhelming and Beth leaned forward to slam the door shut again. But before she did I saw a sight I will not forget. There were rows of shelves in the closet with bottles on them that I later learned had been large canning jars. In a farmhouse, this closet might have been called the summer kitchen. The canned foods from some previous summer's crops were stored there. But in this instance, at least some of the jars of home canned vegetables hadn't sealed properly. Some had broken open. Others had fallen from the shelves and shattered.

Initially all of us turned our faces away from the brutal smell as if we had been struck. Then we peered in again. Among the many jars and parts of jars on the head high shelves were white dots glistening in the light from the dining room window. As Beth pushed on the door there was movement inside the closet. Scurrying. Rats. Huge rats. Many, many, many rats lived in that space.

We had discovered the heart of the colony.

I subsequently learned some things about rats. They breed—7 to 10 pups per litter and they can have one litter per month. That is why Public Health departments ask the question, *When does 1 + 1 = 29,560?* That is the number of rats an adult pair and their offspring can produce in one year. Also, rats have a particular smell which is very much like the odor of cats spraying, but it is the rats marking their territory.

Another telltale sign of severe rat infestation is long trails of grease marks on the walls.

Rats prefer to establish their routes through the environment while in contact with physical structures like walls and curbs, rather than out in the open [3]. This behavior is called *thigmophlic* which means touch loving. The residue of dirt and oils from the rats' fur is what makes the marks along their familiar paths; it creates a visual record of their routes.

Hum...*touch loving.* Was that what Beth and I were offering Tera as she lay dying?

---

[3] Howland Jr., George. The Rat Patrol: From the trailer parks of Kent to the sewers of Eastlake, public-health workers are on the job, teaching people to be smarter than rats. Seattle: Seattle Weekly, (August 9-15, 2006).

THINKING BACK

That day was the turning point for me. I continued to help with the sorting and cleaning but more energy was now put into trying to make sense of what had happened to Tera. How had she come to live in such a place? In such a way? This was Madison, for crying out loud.

I thought back to the early years when I had known Tera. She had several cats and a dog then. In more reflections from Beth' letters, she wrote,

> *We learned to love cats at a young age. My father appeared to hate them; a legacy from his mother. On his mother's rare visits, the cats would hear her voice and scatter.*
>
> *Tera had cat pictures pasted down one side of her cupboard. We loved their soft fur and comforting purring. Terry named most of them. Some of the names I remember were Baby Bing, Dixie Lee, Fuzzy Wuzzy, Foolish, Tiger, Gary, Mama Kitty, Christy, Dee Pee, Buglins, Booty and Sneakie.*

Tera loved domesticated animals, especially cats. Surely these rats and mice and squirrels and chipmunks were not living in the house early on. Tera was always neatly dressed, if somewhat earthy. She bathed in the river, I knew, and then in the nearby campground showers at other times. She looked healthy, strong and tanned in a time when being tan meant being fit.

I began to understand why Beth was spending so much of her time reading the journals Tera had written. I asked about them and, though I only read a few excerpts when Beth offered them to me, I saw that Tera had written extensively about every day of her life. Literally every day.

The entire story was there. Pieces began to come together that filled out the picture of this reclusive, shy woman who had been psychologically abused as a child and come to build the life, as she had once explained to me, that was different.

"I don't live like other people," she had said. I did not realize how profoundly true that was. And yet I had the sense Tera was teaching me a critical life lesson.

I wondered if it was her friend's death that had triggered the changes but then realized he had only been dead about two years and the rat and mouse mazes we were uncovering seemed to have been in place for many years. One of the journals gave the clue. It was the new highway and bridge construction that had started the parade of creatures moving into the house. Tera, with her limited income, had not kept the house well sealed or insulated. Well-meaning volunteer groups had tried to help but had only exacerbated the problems. The highway blasting and digging had unearthed creatures—river rats— who found access to Tera's relatively warm space and food sources, and moved in.

In some back corners, we found rattraps. None were set.

Without heat in the house between November 1 and March 1, pipes had frozen which explained the lack of running water and all the water stored on the kitchen counters. The toilet did not work. As we continued to unpack rooms we discovered a basement door. The oldest part of the house—the old summer cabin—had a basement. Tera had scratched a sign, only visible coming up the basement stairs. It read *Rebels on the River*.

The standing water in that basement space came near the top of Tom's boots as he ventured down into the darkness. The furnace was submerged in water, the pilot light long since drowned. And, as was true upstairs, there was no electricity flowing into the basement. Happily.

Tera had a journal that listed every birthday and anniversary event for all the people she knew well or even in passing. She wrote cards for each of these occasions and kept detailed lists of who received which kind of card and when. My name was on the list and behind it a list of all the cards I'd ever received from her—a long list.

There was a journal for plot changes in *As The World Turns* and other soap operas. There was a journal for events in and thoughts about James Dean's life.

There was a medical journal where Tera wrote about the cat bites she had received and what she had done about them. She used various herbs and aspirin to cure herself.

And there were entries alluding to her breast cancer. "Some discomfort in my breast," she wrote in 1996. Years later, there was a detailed explanation of how she was eating moldy bread to cure the discomfort she was feeling. It was logical in her mind. She believed that penicillin was developed from mold on bread and decided that she could receive the healing medicine if she simply ate the medicinal source.

But it was in the journal on her lovers that I learned more about her friend, Hank. Beth read passages to me as we both sat on turned over metal tubs near the knotty pine bookcases, the house cleaning work neglected for the moment—well, actually, many moments. Hank and Tera had met right after Beth had left for Australia as a young woman. Tera had not followed her sister, as had been planned, because of Hank although she wrote that it was Beth's new boyfriend, and future husband, that was the reason. Tera did not want anyone to know about the relationship because Hank was married. There were pages and pages in journal after journal expressing frustration at the fact that her friend hadn't left his family as he promised her. I could see the written journal entries with capital letters and many exclamation points following the hastily and angrily written words (though I did not read more than what Beth read aloud).

Tera had waited for him while they worked together. She had retired very early and waited for him to be with her. She had waited after he retired. She had wanted a family—children and a wedded relationship. She had waited. And he had come; every day at least twice and sometimes three times. He was faithful to her in his way and she, in hers.

She had ranked her life loves and he was near the top of the list, along with James Dean.

His obituary was included in one of the last journal of loves with yellow highlighting marking these words, *...worked with propane gas for 38 years...was a World War II veteran...enjoyed fishing and walking his dog...was a wonderful, loving husband, father, grandfather, great grandfather and friend.*

There was no way Hank's family could not have known about an affair that lasted more than 40 years, I decided. He was a great friend. On the final page of the journal of loves was a birthday card, apparently never mailed. It was addressed to *my friend* and inside was written, "I did not know an 80-year-old could be so sexy."

AUGUST

My name was now crossed off the list of acceptable visitors on the door to Tera's room in the nursing facility. No one enforced the ban though and I still went for short visits to just be with Tera, often silently, when Beth was working at the house or occasionally out with friends. The chemotherapy treatments had become debilitating and, whether it was the cancer or the stalling drugs, Tera was feeling badly most of the time. She agreed to stop the treatments when it was discussed with the Hospice nurse who was now one of the few legitimate visitors.

There was Tera, lying clean in her bed. I knew she loved animals. I had heard people say that rats made good pets and that rats were just squirrels with bad PR. But she could not have loved the numbers of creatures who were living with her and Sami in the house. As we had moved the massive wood pile in the living room, we uncovered squirrel and chipmunk dens. The house must have literally swarmed at night with the creatures while Tera and Sami huddled on their makeshift bed atop the woodpile near the fireplace. In a sense, they were living in the forest even though there was a house around the wild space. I understood Sami's preference for fresh chipmunk over cat food. I understood why, when he bit me, he hung on to my hand and arm waiting for them to convulse in death.

I thought about a life lived the way she had, so fearful of social ostracizing. Here was a woman who had been passed over by so many of us who believed in individualism and spent our days earning money and getting our children to soccer games. Here was a woman who needed the community and yet would not accept help because of the terrible secret she felt she was living.

The terrible secret of loving someone.

Shakespeare tells us that tragedy comes when a person falls as a result of their own actions. By that definition, Tera's tale is a tragedy.

And yet her final days were filled with love from friends and from her beloved sister who held her and laughed with her and shared memories.

***

Beth had been in Wisconsin for nearly three months, since Memorial Day weekend. Her return ticket to West Australia was set for Labor Day weekend. Beth wanted to go home then because she had promised her daughter she would be midwife for her baby's birth. Tera's chemotherapy treatments had been stopped and she was declining quickly. More time had been spent with the house while Tera slept for long parts of each day and night. Beth now slept in the open room next to Tera's at the nursing facility in case her sister awoke and called for her.

Most of the objects of value to the family had been set aside and a moving truck ordered to pick up the furniture and boxes of letters and journals. All was to be moved to the cargo carrier and sent by ship to Australia. Beth insisted that I take some remembrance from the house, as if I could ever forget that summer. But I did so. A small wooden bench sits by the heating vent in the entryway of my house today. One of my cats often sits on it and soaks in the winter warmth, perhaps similarly to the way Tera and Sami once sat in her sunny bay window overlooking the river.

The fourth dumpster had been dragged down the blacktop driveway that was now badly damaged by the enormous weight of the three preceding bins. The log, which had served as a barricade, had long since been flung onto the outside woodpile.

So often I had the feeling we were looking inside Tera's mind as we cleaned the house. Things were methodically sorted. Many were useless or broken. They were kept for what reason? We would find an entire drawer filled with rubber bands or a cupboard bulging with unopened boxes of toothpaste. There were crates of pencils and others with pens. There were areas for throw rugs or magazines or shoes. On the three beds were piles of clothing, all sorted by season and type—skirts, blouses, dresses, slacks, coats. I saw the blanket I had once crocheted. Some of my mother's woolen coats, from the garage sale, were layered in the jacket-pile.

The corner of one bedroom was laced with costume jewelry. In addition to the boxes, some necklaces hung on and around the movable mirrors of an old-fashioned girl's vanity table. I could picture Tera, the nubile girl, who had escaped her narrow childhood and moved to the exciting big city. There she could emulate the movie stars who had always provided her mental and emotional escape.

Among the family photos and journals, which were clearly treasured items for Tera, were pictures of strikingly beautiful Tera wearing exaggerated outfits—a haughty Zelda Fitzgerald look—with baubles and fringe and glitter. She was often standing in her yard by the river or on her shaky dock. There was a glow to her smile and eyes that let me know she was toying with the photographer, her loyal friend, I assume.

The garage was equally crowded but with the car, bicycles, lawn mowers, and boxes. I think most of that was ultimately left in place when Beth returned to Australia and the house was sold.

Two weeks before Labor Day, Beth again told Tera she would be leaving. This time the message got through the fog of pain medication that Hospice was now providing. Tera was dying.

But the three months she had spent with her beloved Beth had clearly been about joy and love.

At the house, our August days were spent shoveling the remaining debris into the final dumpster. Working alone one last day, I swept the living room floor and stood looking at the beauty of the aged cabin with its cherry floors, stone fireplace, built-in knotty pine cabinets and large windows overlooking the river. Sun dappled the floor. Daily the domestic and Canada Geese called from the river's edge but they no longer automatically came toward humans expecting bread.

The place had been separated from the story of Tera's tale.

Labor Day arrived. Beth was scheduled to begin her long flight home the next day. The phone rang early in the morning. Tera had died during the night. Beth delayed her flight and a funeral was arranged quickly. Without her sister, Tera had no need to continue living. But her final words to me, spoken just a few days prior, yet ring clearly.

She said, "I didn't know it would be so soon." Beth's departure? Or death?

Tera had requested that specific music be played at her funeral. It was a pirated copy (sorry Joe) of Joe Weed's *Prairie Lullaby*. The songs are instrumental versions of what he identifies as "…bedtime hits lovingly played on guitar, harmonica, fiddle and dobro."[4] The songs include *Red River Valley, Brahms Lullaby, Rock-a-Bye Baby*, and *Lonesome River*. These old songs framed Tera's idealized dreams, her losses.

For a long time my darling,' I've waited
For the sweet words you never would say
Now at last all my fond hopes have vanished
For they say that you're going away.
(*Red River Valley*)

I sit here alone on the banks of the river
The lonesome wind blows and the water runs high
I can hear a voice call out from out there in the darkness
But I sit here alone too lonesome to cry.
(*Lonesome River*)

Tom was able to sell Tera's house quickly. I assumed it would be torn down because the odors had only slightly faded with all the work we had done. But no. The new owner gutted the structure and remodeled it. None of us had been able to clean out the summer kitchen closet area where the rats were headquartered. I don't need to know the rest of that story.

Tera's settled estate was worth over a quarter million dollars that happily did not go for cat care.

---

[4] Weed, Joe. Prairie Lullaby. Highland Records, 1993.

THE FINALE

A few weeks later Tera's ashes were ready to be picked up at the funeral home. Beth was back in Australia with her new granddaughter. The small group of friends, including attorney Tom, had been asked to spread Tera's ashes near her river house.

We met just before dawn on a Sunday morning. Three of us stood in Tera's yard, near the house. As we began opening the box of ashes, the Canada Geese and ducks waddled up on the shore. They gathered, at first cawing and then standing silently around the box, muttering as they do. It felt like a tribute to Tera.

We suddenly realized they would think Tera's ashes were food if we spread them there on the river bank, though that wouldn't have been altogether bad.

But then we looked at the bridge. The bridge that had caused so much trauma in Tera's life. It seemed fitting that her final act would be to leave that bridge behind her.

There was no traffic on the highway. So, as the eastern sky began to turn pink, we took the white plastic box onto the bridge. We faced west and began to pour the ashes into the river. There was just enough breeze that the first of the ashes to spill downward came floating back into our faces and open mouths. I had to laugh in spite of the discomfort. A message from Tera; perhaps she now knew we had had her cat euthanized. Sami wasn't a stud cat after all.

We walked across the bridge and poured the ashes into the river on the east side. There was enough light to see the pale remains spread out across the water surface.

Following the slow current, they formed a clearly visible J shape. They looked like a soft curl in long blond hair.

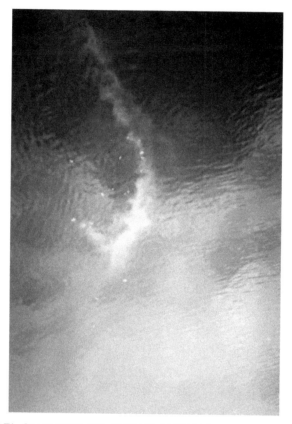

REBEL ON THE RIVER, TERA'S ASHES SPREAD IN RIVER

The American theoretical physicist, John Archibald Wheeler has written,

> *To my mind there must be, at the bottom of it all, not an equation, but an utterly simple idea. And to me that idea, when we finally discover it, will be so compelling, so inevitable, that we will say to one another, Oh, how beautiful. How could it have been otherwise?*[5]

I think Tera knew instinctively, intuitively, what that simple idea was for her and maybe for all of us.

---

[5] Templeton, Sir John & R. Herrmann. *Is God the Only Reality: Science Points to a Deeper Meaning of Universe.* Pennsylvania: Templeton Foundation, 1994..

She lived it in her connections with nature, with the two-leggeds and the four-leggeds.

She lived it with her friend and friends, and with her sister.

She lived it with her belief in the beauty of the romantic life and devoted family she so long sought after and treasured.

The refrain that seemed to tie this together was the simple idea. The utterly simple idea she knew and taught us was the supremacy of love.

So simple.

So very simple.

Love one another.

TERA'S TEACHINGS

Last summer quack grass took over my garden, stretching its rhizomes. Now, loosening and pulling up the runners is a tedious yet unhurried deliberate process. Dig the moist spring dirt for a foot or so around each plant cluster. Gently ease the fragile roots out, pulling with care, hesitating when there is resistance. Break the long root and new grass will grow from each piece. On my knees in the warming soil, I dig and pull, dig and tug, dig and ease out; reflecting back to the summer of Tera. All she wanted was a normal life and yet she was not an ordinary person. She lived in fairy tales.

In my life, I have always tended toward racing about. Doing. Curious. Always moving. (I may be part chipmunk.) Tera's pace was slower. She did not rip past the roses or trample the crab grass. She paused in her quiet way and reflected. She had her bounty of journals. She had her duck and goose companions, her pets, her friend. As she was consciously aware, she did not live like others of this world.

For many people, Tera was the other. Her dreams were conventional—family and hearth—her choices were not. She was one of the fringe people we often simply do not see as we wiz past.

Tera and Beth helped me slowdown that summer. And now, later, I am still more conscious of pace and attention. I continue to reflect on their lessons as I methodically pry rhizomes from spring soil. I visualize Beth's compassionate hands so tenderly touching and massaging Tera's feet and shoulders. Authentic. Honest. Loving. I remember the sisters giggling as their long-submerged memories were refreshed. I reflect on the kindness and love I felt in that darkened stifling room where they so regularly sat huddled together for that final summer of Tera's life.

Can it be so very simple, as Wheeler suggests? Love one another. I'm still pondering.

WHAT IS HOARDING?

Hoarding is defined as *"…the persistent difficulty discarding or parting with possessions, regardless of their actual value. The behavior usually has deleterious effects—emotional, physical, social, financial, and even legal [like eviction]—for a hoarder and family members."*[6]

A person who is a hoarder acquires so many objects that spaces in the home or apartment (or garage, yard, basement, car or even storage areas) can no longer be used as originally intended. The person cannot eat in a dining area, sleep in a bedroom, or even have a chair to sit on, much less invite others over to visit. Tera's south-facing riverside window-seat, was the one place she and Sami could sit in her home. In the winter, there could have been a degree of warmth there, on sunny days.

I honestly did not realize that Tera was one of the estimated (minimum) three million Americans (possibly 1 in 20) who have a hoarding disorder. As I've read more about disposophobia, or compulsive hoarding, I can identify other co-occurring aspects she faced. She was socially isolated, reclusive and lived alone. She was anxious around people until she developed trust, which could take years. She was indecisive and extremely distractible (undiagnosed ADHD or ADD?). She may have been depressed at times and certainly so when she was ill. She did believe the things she acquired could someday be useful or needed even though they likely would only be placed in a box or compartment with other similar found objects. And from my reading, it appears there are often links between hoarding and Obsessive Compulsive Disorder (OCD). Hoarding can also be associated with other health problems such as dementia,

[6] *Hoarding: The Basics.* Anxiety and Depression Association of America. https://adaa.org/understanding-anxiety/obsessive-compuslive-disorder-ocd/hoarding-basics

alcohol/drug misuse, schizophrenia, bipolar disorder, learning disabilities, and autism.[7]

People who hoard may have difficulty organizing their things. A central difference between collecting and hoarding is whether the items are put out on display. But the emotional responses to either of these acquisitions of things may be joy and delight with getting new items, particularly if the possessions (or animals) bring comfort.

A person who hoards may feel the objects they keep and cherish have feelings—human-like qualities. These items can also fill emotional needs for the person. For some, being surrounded by possessions they cannot part with brings a sense of safety, of security. The items may remind them of happier (or safer) times or represent beloved people in their past. There can be a fear that getting rid of the treasured things could lead to losing the memory of that loved person (or animal). Buried beneath the clothing and other items in Tera's home was furniture from her childhood home. The family dining room table. The vanity dresser where Tera put on her movie-star jewelry. Dishes from the farm. Her aunt's rocking chair.

There can be an unreasonable sense of the value given to many of the saved items, though hoarders may call themselves *thrifty* and deny their collecting is a problem. The objects hoarded are often paper (mail, letters, newspapers, photographs, boxes, books), but can also include clothing, plastic bags, household supplies, garbage or food (bread for the ducks in Tera's case), and more.

Some people collect animals with the intention of saving them only to end up with too many to properly maintain and care for.

Personal hygiene and bathing may be an issue as was the case for Tera. She would "go swimming" in the river in the warmer months, but during other seasons there was no running water, heat or electricity in her home to facilitate personal care. And to repair any of these utilities or appliances in the house would have meant allowing strangers to enter the space. Tera was unwilling to do that. She was aware that Beth (and family) did not approve of the state of her home when she wrote that Beth was coming to torch the house. She felt ashamed, and yet did not, or could not, stop accumulating.

---

[7] Smith, K; L. Drummond; S. Ahmed; & J. Bolton. Hoarding. England: Royal College of Psychiatrists Public Education, April 2016.

Over time, the person may be bound in, literally and figuratively, as objects fill spaces. Hoarders can end up leading smaller and smaller lives. In the book *Homer and Langley*, E. L. Doctorow identifies how each brother ended up living in a *cell of space* as more and more passages were blocked in their house. Doctorow describes Langley as "morbidly thrifty."[8] The Collyer brothers, whose real story is the basis of Doctorow's book, faced the kinds of complications that often come with hoarding such as increased risks of falls, injury from shifting or falling items and family conflicts.

Hoarding disorder has been segmented into five levels. Tera's behavior fit in the fifth and most intense level which is identified as including rodent infestation, the kitchen and bathroom being unusable, and disconnected electrical and/or water service.

The Clutter-Hoarding Scale[9] identifies Level V as including the following:

STRUCTURE & ZONING ISSUES	PETS & RODENTS	HOUSEHOLD FUNCTIONS	SANITATION & CLEANLINESS
Structural damage obvious in home Broken walls No electrical power No water connections Sewer septic system non-operational Standing water in basement or room Fire hazardous materials or contaminants exceed local ordinances	Pets dangerous to occupants and/or guests Rodents evident and in sight Mosquito or insect infestations Regional "critter" infestations	Kitchen and bathroom unusable due to clutter Client sleeping elsewhere as house is not livable	Human defecation Rotting food More than 15 aged canned goods with buckled tops and sides

[8] Doctorow, E.L. *Homer & Langley*. New York: Random House, 2009.
[9] The NSGCD Clutter Hoarding Scale: Official Organizational Assessment Tool. Institute for Challenging Disorganization. www.challengingdisorganization.org

Researchers have identified possible causes for hoarding behaviors.

The tendency may be genetic and many hoarders have family members with similar leanings. Beth wrote that she and her mother were also hoarders, but not to the extent Tera was. This environmental exposure was part of the girls' childhoods. Sometimes hoarding is used to keep people away. Could that have been part of the family experience on the farm where they felt so socially estranged? It is important to recognize that no one sets out to intentionally become a hoarder.

Stress or emotional triggers like grief can exacerbate hoarding behaviors. Tera fought with her inability to achieve her dream of marriage and family—like what Beth had accomplished. Tera's ranting at Hank may have been a measure of her emotional stress at not achieving that goal. Additionally, she had chosen to put her hopes in Hank's hands, figuratively, when she opted not to follow Beth to Australia as had been the original girlhood plan. He was not able to come through for her in the ways she dreamed of even though he was faithful with her for forty years.

Grief over a traumatic event or serious loss can lead to worsening hoarding behavior. Hank's death was surely traumatic. Tera's dreams were permanently lost.

Also, hoarding appears to be a brain-based disorder and it may turn out that genetics are the major cause. Hoarding fills an emotional need. It has also been shown that those who cannot de-clutter have unique brain activity that is distinct from people with typical OCD (obsessive compulsive disorder) although there can be connections between these two conditions for about 20% of hoarders. There is excessive activity in the anterior cingulate cortex—the brain region involved with decision making—when a hoarder is faced with giving up their acquisitions.[10]

It appears that, as research suggests, Tera's hoarding increased with age. The average age of onset is 13 but symptoms increase with age.

---

[10] Szalavitz, M. *Inside the Hoarder's Brain: A Unique Problem with Decision Making.* hppt://healthlandtime. com/2012/08/07/inside-the-hoarders-brain-a-unique-problem-with-decision-making, 10/2/12.

Scientists do not suggest cleaning out a hoarder's things, which could lead to mistrust and anger. The person may be living with a fear that others could throw away their treasures or take them without permission. The objects may well make the person feel safer. It is also likely any spaces that are cleared out will quickly be refilled.

Suggested responses include:

- Educate yourself about Compulsive Hoarding Syndrome
- Participate in and encourage the treatment process (involving extended family or friends)
- Be open to understanding, compassion and patience
- Do not get into arguments; it will not help the situation
- Be aware of your non-verbal expressions of dismay or disagreement
- Don't suggest what the person should do or not do; this condition requires professional therapy
- Acknowledge accomplishments for steps that are taken
- Remember that the hoarded environment did not occur overnight and will not be immediately fixed
- Remember too that if the individuals could stop their behavior and clean up or throw away items, they would. They cannot do so.[11]

Self-assessment questions can also be raised by the person who is hoarding, or others. These include:

1. Do I have a plan to use this item?
2. Have I used it this past year?
3. How many of these do I have?
4. Do I feel emotionally attached to this item; for example, does it have sentimental value to me?

---

[11] The Compulsive Hoarding Center. The Anxiety Treatment Center. http://anxietytreatmentexperts.com/compuslive-hoarding-center/

The Saving Inventory-Revised is a self-report measure of hoarding commonly used:

(http://www.ocfoundation.org/uploadedfiles/hoarding/resources/si-r(modified format).pdf [12]

And, suggestions for treatment approaches are identified at The Anxiety Treatment Center.[13]

---

[12] Grisham, J & P. Baldwin. Hoarding disorder cutting through the clutter. Medicine Today, (Vol 16, No. 9), September, 2015.
[13] OCD and Anxiety Disorders are treatable conditions. The Anxiety Treatment Center. http://anxietytreatmentexperts.com/compulsive-hoarding-center/

DISCUSSION QUESTIONS

Book clubbers, read on... *Tera's Tale* is your next book! A memoir, it raises life questions for us to address, in community, among friends.

We learn from each other's life journeys: the decision points, the joys, sorrows, struggles and impacts of socially constructed, societal mores, Tera fully lived all of these. She teaches us in that special way she had. Many people collect objects. Some tip over the edge into hoarding, as Tera did. The difference? Collectors are proud to show off their collections. Hoarders, not so much. Tera was a shy, reclusive hoarder. And so very much more.

1) In what ways have your childhoods impacted who you have become?

2) We are surrounded by cultural rules. How do we decide which ones to follow, and when? And why?

3) How could we interact with "the other" more authentically— the person whose life experience is so very different than our own?

4) What is pure joy in our lives? Sorrow? Fear?

5) How do we deal with losing that thing we spent a lifetime pursuing? How do we help another deal with such a loss?

6) Would you have assisted with the house clearing, despite rats? Why? Why not?

7) Is it as simple as "love one another"?

8) *Tera fantasized about the societal dream of marriage and family.* Tera was a romantic who perpetuated her mother's beliefs about idealized women's roles. Were these beliefs a gift for Tera? A tragedy? Other?

9) *And then I felt the fear that I was to feel repeatedly in the coming months. I don't know exactly what it was. A fear that the disease would spread to me? A fear of seeing Tera in uncontrolled pain? A fear of the unknown of what lay ahead? A fear of death?* How would you have responded to Tera's cancer diagnosis? What would you have done? Why?

10) *Clearly, Beth needed help and she took what I thought was a courageous path and one that assured my loyalty. She asked for my help.* Would you have committed to help Beth? Why? Why not?

11) *But Beth saw a completely different reality. For her, the house contained a plethora of childhood memories...Family treasures were hidden like nuggets among the piles.* Would you have worked to recover the family heirlooms from the house, even amid the chaos?

12) *Did Tera's inability to live her dream lead to what was uncovered in her house?* Could Tera's inability to control her dreams have led to (or exacerbated) the hoarding?

13) *As a person almost obsessive about cleanliness and neatness, was I sickened or disgusted by Tera's house in ways I could not address or admit to? Was I judging her?* How do we avoid blaming *the victim* of a disease like hoarding?

14) *Tera lived with the* terrible secret *of loving someone.* In some other cultures, having more than one wife, more than one lover, is acceptable. Is that wrong?

15) *To my mind there must be, at the bottom of it all, not an equation, but an utterly simple idea. And to me that idea, when we finally discover it, will be so compelling, so inevitable, that we will say to one another, Oh, how beautiful. How could it have been otherwise?*[14] Is "love one another" that simple idea?

---

[14] Templeton, Sir John & R. Herrmann. Is God the Only Reality: Science Points to a Deeper Meaning of Universe. Pennsylvania: Templeton Foundation, 1994.

ABOUT THE AUTHOR

Her work experiences prove the adage that a career is something we look back on and only then understand. Judy's first job was in adult education with a northeastern Iowa community college. From there she moved to Madison College and then completed her Ph.D. in adult education at the University of Wisconsin-Madison. Judy retired from teaching at Edgewood College in the fall of 2018 and is proud to have published three books: *Because I Am Jackie Millar, In Warm Blood: Prison & Privilege, Hurt & Heart,* and now *Tera's Tale: Rebel on the River.* She lives next to Tera's river, Madison, with her husband and big-boned cat, Rufus. You may contact her at judadrian@gmail.com.

CPSIA information can be obtained
at www.ICGtesting.com
Printed in the USA
FSHW020222050319
56091FS